where abouts

where

SUSANNA SIREFMAN

abouts

NEW ARCHITECTURE WITH LOCAL IDENTITIES

Foreword by George Ranalli
Essay by Michael Sorkin

THE MONACELLI PRESS

This book was published in conjunction with the exhibition "Whereabouts: New Architecture with Local Identities" at the School of Architecture, Urban Design and Landscape Architecture at City College, City University of New York.

The author, the publisher, and the School of Architecture, Urban Design and Landscape Architecture would like to thank the National Endowment for the Arts and the Graham Foundation for Advanced Studies in the Fine Arts for their generous support of this book.

First published in the United States of America in 2004 by
The Monacelli Press, Inc.
902 Broadway, New York, New York 10010.

Library of Congress Cataloging-in-Publication Data
Sirefman, Susanna.
Whereabouts : new architecture with local identities / Susanna Sirefman ;
foreword by George Ranalli ; essay by Michael Sorkin.
p. cm.
Published in conjunction with an exhibiton held at the School of Architecture, Urban Design and Landscape Architecture at City College, City University of New York.
ISBN 1-58093-120-0
1. Architecture—United States—20th century—Exhibitions. 2. Architecture—United States—21st century—Exhibitions. 3. Regionalism in architecture—United States—Exhibitions. I. Sorkin, Michael, 1948– . II. City University of New York. City College. School of Architecture, Urban Design and Landscape Architecture. III. Title.
NA712.S57 2004   720'.973'0747471—dc22   2003020163

Printed and bound in Italy

Designed by Esther Bridavsky

Cover: Shim-Sutcliffe Architects, Island House; photograph by James Dow

8   FOREWORD **George Ranalli**

10   WHEREABOUTS **Susanna Sirefman**

19   WITH THE GRAIN **Michael Sorkin**

NORTH   29   Shim-Sutcliffe Architects

51   Brian MacKay-Lyons Architecture Urban Design

SOUTH   75   Rick Joy Architects

93   Wendell Burnette Architects

EAST   111   Wesley Wei Architects

135   SHoP: Sharples Holden Pasquarelli

WEST   153   Kuth/Ranieri Architects

169   Lubowicki/Lanier Architects

184   Biographies

190   Illustration Credits

TO ZANDER AND SARAH

ACKNOWLEDGMENTS

Several people and institutions were instrumental in making this book possible. I would first like to thank George Ranalli, dean of the City College of New York School of Architecture, for providing the inspiration and impetus for this project and for his terrific mentorship. Thanks to Mark Robbins, former director of design at the National Endowment for the Arts, and his team and to Richard Solomon, director of the Graham Foundation for Advanced Studies in the Fine Arts in Chicago, for financing both this book and the exhibition that preceded it. I am especially grateful to the provost of City College, Ziv Deegan, who matched our grant funds. A special thanks to architects David Childs, Stanley Tigerman, and Tom Beeby for believing in my proposal.

A huge thank you to editor extraordinaire Andrea Monfried, who proposed expanding the original scope of the book, and to graphic designer Esther Bridavsky, who has a marvelous eye. I appreciate the cooperation of the architects, who were remarkably generous with their time and materials, and the many photographers, who allowed us to publish their striking images.

An enormous thanks to the Sirefmans: without my mom, Carol, this book would not have been feasible; fortunately, my dad, Josef, did not mind Mom's constant baby-sitting duty. I am grateful to my erudite, architecture-loving husband Alexander Shapiro for his encouragement and for providing a fine example of intellectual rigor. Finally, thanks to my daughter, Sarah Eleanor Shapiro, who makes everything, including the sport of looking at buildings and how we live in them, seem so worthwhile.

FOREWORD: GEORGE RANALLI

It is the role of the academy to support and encourage new talent as
it emerges. The eight architectural firms invited to participate in
"Whereabouts: New Architecture with Local Identities" at the School of
Architecture, Urban Design and Landscape Architecture at City College,
City University of New York, have recently established practices and
produced extraordinary projects in their respective locations. These
architects enrich their work with both a respect for and a response to
the environmental characteristics of their particular regions. In addition, the designs are executed with a sophisticated level of artistry that
demands a focused reading.

A new synthetic, emotionally engaged, investigative, and inventive architecture needs to be formulated as a symbol of the change in thought
taking place at the beginning of the twenty-first century. This architecture will establish linkages between landscapes of urbanism and geography and respond to the necessity of energy efficiency while still explor-
ing the relationship between form and material construction.

The study of preexisting architectural projects is an important educa-
tional tool. Each generation of architects is drawn to reexamine the
theoretical underpinnings of other bodies of work—historic and current,
local and distant. Buildings hold a vital link to both time and place, and
the projects in this book connect not only to their particular environ-

ments but to the continuum of architecture and architectural thought as a whole: they demonstrate an intense and provocative relationship between the historical associations of the site, the climatic conditions of the area, the technical development of the design, and the nature of the construction method.

Conscious of their time, these architects utilize the present moment, connect to contemporary culture and material production, and work toward a sensitive, aesthetic reinterpretation of time and space. Whether a design is in the rugged, sparse, and internally oriented North, the intellectual and historically rooted East, the more experimental West, or the sun- and heat-saturated South, it evidences an intimate communication with the urban or landscape setting and suggests that the architects have created something completely original.

Architecture should not be mimetic, producing a likeness of an adjacent building or earth form, but should be a measured, careful, intuitive, and gestural response, filtered through abstraction and artistry. Structures are connected to site by emotional contact with the feeling of the environment, not simply by looking for and copying available forms, be they human-made or organic. The cues present in the environment, the needs of the client, and the personal touch of the architect make a building not simply functional but a work of art.

WHEREABOUTS: SUSANNA SIREFMAN

Architecture has long been associated with history, tradition, time, and place. These preoccupations have been transformed into built form in a multitude of different ways by centuries of architects. Yet much of modern architecture, from 1900 on, sought to universalize design. Less importance was placed on local conditions—climate, topography, or indigenous construction techniques—than on formal design conventions. Today, much urban architecture seems interchangeable from city to city and country to country, while far too much suburban design consists of homogenous, cookie-cutter, neotraditional housing. Moreover, the latest digital technologies and information networks in our now global world have the potential to further disassociate architecture from place. Perhaps in response to this situation, there is a growing undercurrent across North America in the opposite direction—an exciting resurgence of interest in the architectural reinvention of place.

The body of work presented in this book is refreshing proof of this new trend. Each of these designs, influenced by a particular amalgamation of local circumstances, fits rather specifically in its own location. Salient regional qualities—construction techniques, materials, cultural idioms—have not vanished; rather, they are reimagined, redefined. Local climate, geography, topology, sociology, and psychology all play an important part. Each of the conventional regions of North America—North, South, East, and West—is represented by two firms to offer a broad understanding of what it means to build in different parts of North America.

The selected architects are relatively young—mostly under fifty. Their built work is in general modest in scale and program. It is the rare American architect who builds a large-scale civic project or skyscraper before the age of fifty; as a result, all but four of the book's eighteen projects are residential. Fortunately, the private domestic dwelling is a rich typology within which to explore architecture's relationship to place and culture. In fact, it is the very scale and intimate nature of house that enables these architects to explore local identity in all of its complexity.

Not surprisingly there is much common ground among the diverse projects. All the architects included are modernists, and all approach their work with an individualistic (though coherent) set of rules. Each values abstraction, precision, and rationalism; each is enamored of the clean rectilinear line and subscribes to a lushly minimalist aesthetic. All the architects included are pragmatists. This does not mean that they are practical. They are pragmatic because they believe in the craft and process of building and the power of the physical realization of their ideas. It is clear that there seems to be some undeclared unity within this generation of architects as to the definition of place. This hidden consensus is not about a universal attitude or a universal answer, or about the requirements of the job. Instead, the shared sensibility is an appreciation of the role place takes in the design process, a commitment to letting the site set the tone for a project. The desire to cultivate and redefine the "genius loci" creates a conspicuous overlap of intention in much of the work. But as each specific place has its own unique spirit, these similar lines of investigation and parallel agendas produce very different results. While some of the underlying principles driving this work are transferable from place to place, the final products are not.

The exploration of the relationship between place and architecture has been a part of architecture throughout history. However, the majority of

Wesley Wei Architects,
Media Residence: front
(north) and back (south)
views

recent (1950s on) writing on the subject, from Christian Norberg-Schulz's 1963 *Intentions in Architecture* to Kenneth Frampton's 1982 essay "Towards a Critical Regionalism," has focused on the culturally symbolic and decorative rather than on the functional and pragmatic. Frampton's pseudo-political manifesto, celebrating regionalism as an *-ism* (under the guise of "critical regionalism," a term coined by Alexander Tzonis and Liane Lefaivre in their essay on the work of Dimitris and Suzana Antonakakis in 1981), demonstrates that Frampton defines architecture as a reflection of time and place. He is primarily concerned with the static or symptomatic representation of local mores and warns architects against "the domination of hegemonic power." In strong contrast to Frampton's view, the work presented here is not architecture as a *reflection of* time and place but architecture that exhibits an ongoing *relationship between* time and place.

Three fundamental ingredients are necessary to design a building: program, site, and invention. Although these elements are independent, individual factors, it is their confluence, their moment of overlap, that informs a building's design. Program encompasses the activities and events that will occur within the building. No matter how fluid or flexible these activities are, any particular building typology is primarily defined by them. Site, the location for the project, affects everything about a building, from basic orientation on a plot of land and potential zoning possibilities to the smallest aspect of detailing. An architect's act of invention, her idea or ideas about a project, is the least tangible element in the act of creation. A designer's training, personal preoccupations, relationship to the client, and design process are all part of the simmering brew. The identity and attitudes of a project's main players—the architect, the client, the intended user—provide an important ingredient in the mix. Local culture and local economics usually determine who the client is and what sort of architect might be selected. This thereby predetermines much of the project's potential.

NORTH The two architectural firms representing the North—Shim-Sutcliffe Architects and Brian MacKay-Lyons Architecture Urban Design—both hail from Canada. The former is based in Toronto; the latter in Halifax, Nova Scotia. Canada's rugged natural landscape and demanding climate inform much of their work. Proud self-declared pragmatists, the architects at both firms have a strong interest in the local culture of the everyday.

The two projects by Shim-Sutcliffe, a townhouse in Stratford and a retreat on Howe Island in the St. Lawrence River, juxtapose the differing design issues that occur in urban and rural settings. The townhouse is a study in vertical design; the summer retreat is an exploration of the horizontal. Fiercely loyal to indigenous building techniques in both city and country, the firm employed local Mennonite builders to frame the townhouse and chose a concrete usually found in barn foundations for the summer house. Both designs are tight, insular compositions: the wintry climate dictates an internal focus. Island House, a vacation home for two sailing buffs, is located smack in the middle of a pasture. Merging landscape and building, the architects extended the meadow by planting the two low rooftops of the house with colorful wildflowers. However, the rooftop of the only double-height space—the living room—is not planted and stands out as a beacon against the landscape. Nestled into the terrain, this low-lying building is partially protected from the harsh northern winter.

Brian MacKay-Lyons
Architecture Urban Design,
Wicht-MacNeill Cottage:
drawing and stair view

Brian MacKay-Lyons, founder and principal of Brian MacKay-Lyons Architecture Urban Design, was born, raised, and trained in Halifax. The austere weather and severe geography of the city, along with MacKay-Lyons's interest in agrarian and maritime building types (cottage, shed, barn, and outbuildings), result in simple, clean structures that are both modern and historical. The typical shingled farmhouses of Nova Scotia are spartan, simple envelopes focused around fireplaces. This has become a part of MacKay-Lyons's grammar, as in the Howard House, essentially a long tube punctuated with totemic elements: well, hearth, truss, and south-facing window. The "rough and ready" metal cladding around the building is in keeping with the fishing cove context. House #22 and the Danielson Cottage are both pairs of houses, two detached volumes connected by walkways, that recall the local outbuilding tradition. All three projects employ traditional boat-building techniques.

An advocate for what he describes as the "democratization of architecture," MacKay-Lyons likens his design interest in the vernacular to the "anthropologist who studies ordinary pots and pans." This architect has been so inspired by local folk art techniques that for the design-development phase of the Wicht-MacNeill Cottage in Kingsburg, Nova Scotia (1989), he drew stylized sections that resemble local folk paintings. This acceptance of the local culture, conventions, and vernacular as a point of view carries over into what MacKay-Lyons calls the "folk-tech" built aspect of his work.

SOUTH The importance of engaging a site's vistas from within drives the work of architects from all regions. Both Rick Joy Architects and Wendell Burnette Architects, the two firms representing the South, are based in Arizona and have had the good fortune to build on spectacular desert sites: Rick Joy Architects in the Tucson Mountains and Wendell Burnette Architects in the Echo Mountain foothills outside of Phoenix.

The exploitation of light and view was so important to Rick Joy, founder of Rick Joy Architects, in Casa Jax that the project exploded into three freestanding volumes, each facing a different direction, thus marrying "perfect view" and "perfect time of day." The interiors were designed around these framed moments, creating a house that also functions as a desert sundial. Joy's Tubac House also makes much of panoramic mountain-range vistas. Expansive glazing, strategically placed courtyards, and protruding steel box forms penetrate the building in carefully selected but seemingly random locations to frame specific views.

There is a wonderfully playful quality to the siting and design of the Tubac House. The approach is via a gravel road. Sound is important to Joy—he believes the unexpected crunch of gravel in the desert heightens a visitor's awareness of the surroundings. Weathered steel swathes the house in rusty planes, a departure from Joy's usual rammed-earth buildings. (He built his early reputation constructing buildings in Arizona out of desert soil, a traditional southwestern material.) Reminiscent of rusty debris and ancient railroad ties, this shimmery, copper cladding also suggests both the Wild West and the orange mountains in the background.

Like the projects by Shim-Sutcliffe Architects, the work by Wendell Burnette Architects juxtaposes the various design issues characteristic of urban and suburban settings. The Tocker Residence, although located next to a busy road in a suburb of Phoenix, takes full advantage of a sensational view of both mountains and city. The house looks onto a panorama of downtown Phoenix against the Sierra Estrella range. Principal Wendell Burnette's urban studio for David Michael Miller Associates in Scottsdale, Arizona, is on a well-traveled block surrounded by cafés, galleries, and furniture shops. This design is driven by views not outward but inward—by the task of bringing light into the building. Desert light, even in a city setting, is intense and tricky to control. Burnette uses wonderful techniques—strategically placed vertical slots for windows, thinly sliced Indian onyx instead of glass—learned during his apprenticeship at Frank Lloyd Wright's Taliesin West.

Building in the South and the West is entirely different from building in the East. Yankee culture—practical, conservative, risk-averse, and often litigious—sadly prevents many younger architects from building and experimenting. Although there is a plethora of young talent in New York, Boston, and Philadelphia, it is difficult to find talented, site-sensitive architects under fifty with interesting buildings (of any scale) on the East Coast. Young eastern firms, not by choice but by happenstance, design mostly interiors, both residential and commercial.

New York–based SHoP is typical. The office has completed only a few projects: Mitchell Park in Greenport, Long Island, and a temporary installation for P.S.1 Contemporary Art Center. However, the firm is becoming well known for yet-to-be-realized projects such as the Museum of Sex and Light Bridges, both in New York. Philadelphia-based Wesley Wei Architects, founded in 1987, designs an interesting mix of interiors and small buildings. On the East Coast, the lengthier nature of an architect's apprenticeship (again by necessity and not by choice), combined with the idea of the East as the nation's intellectual epicenter, has resulted in a more theoretical approach to design. Although there are many exceptions to this rule throughout North America, both SHoP and Wesley Wei Architects devote significant time to initial research and schematic design processes.

Principal Wesley Wei creates elaborate, poetic narratives for each element of a project and explores these metaphor-rich chronicles through exquisite collages, analytic sections, and numerous models. His process includes an ongoing study of formal and sequential sections resulting in a rich physical, visual, and programmatic layering in his projects, each of which has a unique, self-referential vocabulary. SHoP, on the other hand, is enamored of computer software as a form-generating process. Typical of recent graduates of the Columbia School of Architecture, partners Chris, Bill, and Coren Sharples, Kim Holden, and Gregg Pasquarelli label climatic, topological, and demographic properties as "fields of influence, variegated fronts, vector forces and ambient flows." Despite this semantic obfuscation, they are committed to recording, analyzing, and addressing existing site conditions. The Mitchell Park master plan demonstrates an appreciation of the idea of connection. After a relentless "tactical mapping" of automobile and pedestrian traffic flows, sun patterns, tides, and the movement of boats and outsiders, the architects began to weave the site back into the village it borders. Issues of view and visibility take on a particular twist in the work of Wesley Wei, appropriate to the vari-

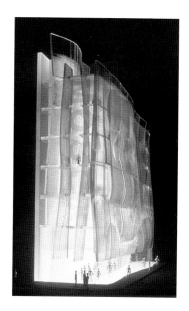

SHoP: Sharples Holden Pasquarelli, Museum of Sex: Model view

able climate and conservative nature of the East. The Media House, in Pennsylvania, was commissioned by an immensely private art collector. Masking the view into the house from the surrounding property and maintaining a sense of acute seclusion informed Wei's design.

WEST

The West Coast presents an entirely different context: it has long been a haven of tolerance for self-invention and social diversity. This has made for a culture receptive to innovative architecture that offers fertile grounds for young architects. Certainly avant-garde architecture and architects have long characterized Southern California: Greene & Greene, Irving Gill, Frank Lloyd Wright, Rudolph Schindler, Richard Neutra, Charles and Ray Eames, John Lautner, and Frank Gehry. San Francisco, although considerably more conservative than Los Angeles in matters of contemporary design, is refreshingly open-minded nonetheless. The tradition of the bohemian architect in San Francisco is a long-standing one, dating back to Bernard Maybeck, who designed the city's Palace of Fine Arts (1913–15). Two California firms, Lubowicki/Lanier Architects, based in Los Angeles, and Kuth/Ranieri Architects, based in San Francisco—both run by husband-and-wife teams—build innovative, rational buildings.

Lubowicki/Lanier Architects,
O'Neill Guest House:
Kit-of-parts model views

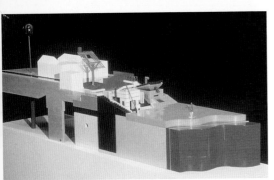

Principals Paul Lubowicki and Susan Lanier develop stories, intricate narratives with a distinctly Hollywood twist, as a design tool. For the O'Neill Guest House near Wilshire Boulevard, the architects were inspired by the work of cartoonist George Herriman. His "Krazy Kat" comic strips exemplify the complex interpersonal relationships the designers hope to capture in their architecture. Lubowicki/Lanier explored Herriman's graphic techniques—layering a number of stories into one strip, for instance, or "bubble" strips within the main strip—in a series of silk screens about program, site, and design for the guest house. The project ultimately became about the building as a collection of parts in an intricate dialogue with one another.

Just as locale offers an infinite variety of influences, any one aspect of a building can develop a multitude of relationships with these elements on many different levels. The facade of the Iann/Stolz Residence designed by Byron Kuth and Liz Ranieri is one example. The composition incorporates typical Bay Area conventions—bay window, front-facing garage door, and street-side roof deck—but the skin of the building probes for a deeper connection to its site. San Francisco is a white city, with Mediterranean qualities of light. The Victorian houses, pastel and encrusted with decorative woodwork, that line many streets create a filigree of shadow and a sieve for the evening fog in the Bay Area. Kuth/Ranieri used the contradictions of surface and depth to reinterpret the envelope of the Iann/Stolz Residence as an armature for light. Across the facade, undulating mahogany slats become smaller as they rise from the ground, while the battens in between become closer and deeper. Like Brian MacKay-Lyons, Kuth/Ranieri borrowed building techniques from other industries. The Iann/Stolz facade is constructed with a board-and-batten method that borrows from shipbuilding technology.

In the first century BC, Marcus Vitruvius Pollio, the great Roman architect and engineer, described rather romantically "The Origin of the Dwelling House" in his *Ten Books on Architecture:*

Therefore it was the discovery of fire that originally gave rise to the coming together of men, to the deliberative assembly, and to social intercourse. And so, as they kept coming together in greater numbers into one place, finding themselves naturally gifted beyond the other animals in not being obliged to walk with faces to the ground, but upright and gazing upon the splendour of the starry firmament, and also in being able to do with ease whatever they chose with their hands and fingers, they began in that first assembly to construct shelters. Some made them of green boughs, others dug caves on mountainsides, and some, in imitation of the nests of swallows and the way they built, made places of refuge out of mud and twigs. Next, by observing the shelters of others and adding new detail to their own inceptions, they constructed better and better kinds of huts as time went on.

Like Vitruvius's statement, the projects included here were created through a delicate balance of imagination, careful observation, and an understanding of local precedent. Each building possesses a timeless and sustainable quality, a characteristic particularly important in the twenty-first century. Extremely modern, honest and precise in their relationship to place, these examples of contemporary architecture display a connection that is ancient and traditional.

What makes architecture particular? The possibility of building anything anywhere is architecture's greatest crisis and challenge. Fear of the homogenizing reach of globalization leads to a search for local architectures—the contemporary rethinking of place. The role of the profession in the production of such styles of authenticity is under tremendous attack from the cultural command-and-control system of global capital.

Can architecture resist this? Today's reverence for yesterday's authenticity yields mainly preservationism, our dominant ideology of urban form making. Preservationism embodies an idea about urbanity that puts special emphasis on the physical and the historical, predicated on the potential irreplaceability of architectural objects and spaces. Such judgments are subject to tremendous vagaries because of the inevitable fluctuations of taste. Victorian architecture, for example, once reviled, is now beloved. To make such assessments, preservationists distill the past and its traditions into a negotiable set of all too simple signifiers.

This view becomes an urbanism—or a regionalism—when it is concluded that a set of practices is successful enough to merit not simply protection but expansion. The current rubric for this is "contextualism."

Contextualism produces, on one hand, historic districting that sanctions only alterations and additions with a more or less articulate theory of fit and, on the other, a glut of vaguely historical architectures in non-historic contexts, a downside of Tudor McDonald's outlets and neoclassical doodads on the fronts of suburban condos. The upside should be respect.

Alas, most preservationism offers a neutron-bomb style of respect, preserving the object but oblivious to the life, the ecology, that produced it. A more practicable view of contextual urbanism must begin with the recognition—à la Jane Jacobs—of the centrality of the idea of the neighborhood within the city. A close identification between place and community is not only about the physical. The idea of the local also encompasses habits, folkways, friendships, small-scale sets of dependencies, and other negotiated elements of daily life.

An expansion of this view to a larger economic and environmental setting produces a still more invigorated sense of place, one that responds to both the social and the physical. Such an expansion, though, is not perfectly elastic: a biotope proposes its own set of demands. Human lifestyles and consumption are often opposed to the preservation of natural systems. Indeed, global accessibility and Western assumptions of entitlement have created a false idea of the bearing capacity and character of place.

Today, this set of assumptions is under serious critique. Region can exist in many registers: theoretical, temporal, climatic, biological, cultural, and so on. For architects, the approach to such particularities often begins with an idea of mimetic regionalism, an elaboration of historicism via a set of local expressive conventions. Typical is the fake adobe style of the energy-guzzling rancheros in the developer Southwest or the ersatz Colonial Williamsburgs of the new urbanists, primitive and banal co-optations, forms of camouflage and imitation.

However, when the mimetic is expanded to natural as well as cultural landscapes, other possibilities are liberated, creating a larger notion of a natural aesthetic. The glowing tectonic of a mesa at sunrise, the cliff face overlooking the infinite ocean, the dark green of conifers, the undulation of a meadow, a birch white against the snow—all these have immediate translations into architecture.

Yet nature is not predictable, producing forms through complex, looping systems. Imitating nature, the hoariest of artistic motives, suggests—in an environmentally conscious age—that architecture absorbs something of the process rather than simply aping the effects. Such an imitation should consider materials that are abundant in a given place and responsiveness to specifics of climate, both fundamental to any truly successful architecture of locality.

Climate defines regions that cut across cultures, cuing local possibilities in a global context. The tactics of climate control are today commutative: an overhang inspired by South Asia, a windscoop from the Sahara, a thick wall from Africa can migrate as needed. Such techniques of modulation may be distilled to their principles: the grail is passive, machinery-free moderation. Just as the well-watered lawn has ceased to be the acceptable face of human life in the desert, so should a high BTU count be everywhere a last resort.

Architecture must be encouraged to continue the biotope; we manipulate its capacity to our own peril. Working within the biotope is more than a matter of ecological engineering; our demands on the land are also aesthetic. The notion of an "organic" architecture contains an idea of integrity, but also of agency, a kind of terrestrial collaboration.

The specificity of this approach embraces local tradition as a source of ingenious and fitting environmental responses but is also undergirded by an ethical sense—a sense of a shared environment. This ethic is predicated on self-preservation, a generalized love of the planet, a concern for the finitude of resources, and an idea of subjectivity that embraces difference.

Kenneth Frampton has famously suggested "critical regionalism" (a concept originated by Liane Lefaivre and Alexander Tzonis) as the grounds for an "architecture of resistance." For Frampton, this practice lies between the dogmatisms of modernist high-tech and the mendacities of revivalism. He advocates the incorporation of cues from local qualities of light and air, a standard of tactility, and a Heideggerian idea of the boundedness of place in order to "mediate the impact of universal civilization with elements derived indirectly from the peculiarities of a particular place."

Frampton's critical regionalism is the architectural analogue to the neo-liberal politics of Tony Blair's "third way"—a path between the homogenization of modernist technophilia and the dumb recall of culturally irrelevant fantasies of locality. At first blush this seems reasonable. But Frampton's essay also clearly advocates a particular spur of modernism, and his sense of region is symbolic rather than functional. The globalism behind his regionalism is formal; it is not the theory of a deep—or even shallow—ecologist.

Frampton has a predilection for the "natural" and for structural and material honesty, but the quest is fundamentally aesthetic. Jørn Utzon and Alvar Aalto are Frampton's paradigmatic critical regionalists, architects who have over time proposed interesting variations in the relationship to region. Aalto is the double exemplar here. His early work is frankly internationalist. Later, his buildings became more mimetically picturesque, more topographic in their situation, and more engaged with the tactilities of craft. But the work of the two Scandinavians is relatively mute on questions of urbanism, the most revealing arena for the interactions of the architectural, social, and natural. Looking at individual works outside of a context of influence is risky: regionalism in the twenty-first century can be elective, its influence promiscuous. In this sense there is an inevitable double region in all contemporary practice.

Many of the practices included here do begin with a regionalism of subtly abstracted mimetic tectonics. Modernist in their formal lineage, these architects do not explicitly imitate either the landscape or historic architecture; instead they evoke both. All share a sense of unadorned, "natural" materiality. Stained or treated rather than painted and using Cor-Ten steel, masonry, clapboard, plywood, and copper, these buildings are susceptible to weathering, primed to assume an indigenous patina rather than defended against transformation.

Striation is the leading formal signifier of building wedded to the land. This horizontal banding not only expresses the earthly strata of geomorphology but evokes the Wrightian ethic of the horizontal, even in structures—such as Kuth/ Ranieri Architects' Iann Stolz Residence or Lubowicki/Lanier Architects' O'Neill Guest House—in which the overall configuration is cubic or vertical.

The social regionalism of this work, like its formalism, is abstracted. The projects exist in another global cultural region: the terrain of late bourgeois domesticity. The predominant typology in this collection is the house, often the first project for a young practice. But the contemporary house is also a confrontation with anachronism. The 2000 U.S. census reveals that the number of us living in nuclear families has now slipped to 25 percent. But the house can be understood as more than the register of a fading familial arrangement. It is also a basic increment of architecture, a single building housing a foundational social unit. Modernism had a certain ambivalence about the house and expressed a challenge to the nuclear family, not to its existence but to its privileges and pleasures.

For the work of these architects as well as for the rehabilitation of the single-family housing unit, Mies is the progenitor and the Barcelona Pavilion—though emphatically not a residence—the paragon. Here was a space truly reduced to fundamentals, "pure" space functioning on an almost symbolic plane. What stuns about the pavilion is both its ethereal spatial simplicity and its sumptuous materiality: polished stainless, marble, and leather. Mies's contribution to the reinvention of domestic architecture was this reintroduction of materiality into the ambivalent scene of whitewashed modernism. This counterreformation was social as well: in the design of his great country houses, Mies never disdained either received styles of social life or the idea that the house might site everyday luxuries. Like the houses of Mies, those published here pursue not the zero degree of inhabitation but a kind of simplicity. Life unfolds according to reliable stations: bedroom, bath, living room, kitchen. The links between them are simple and direct, and all of these projects seek the efficiency of clear and generative plans.

Brian MacKay-Lyons Architecture Urban Design's Howard House, for example, elongated like a railroad flat, solves circulation without a corridor. Wesley Wei Architects' Media Residence is also compact and simplified, with its dedicated circulation space pared to a stair. Rick Joy Architects' Casa Jax goes this simplification one further, breaking its three primary programmatic elements into separated pavilions, each focused on one view. This strategy (much used by Frank Gehry) constitutes a paradoxical sort of efficiency—the elimination of the spaces of circulation at the price of a less "efficient" envelope. Lubowicki/Lanier pursues this beautifully in the small paired guest cottages of the O'Neill project.

Much of the work here is under the influence of this kind of minimalism, a modesty that also asks to be read environmentally. This is less the reductive styling of the art world or the Miesian paradigm than a remnant of the minimalism of modernity. Miniaturization and attention to the precise deployments of objects within the architectural field is a characteristic intensity of this group of projects and contributes to the lapidary quality of the work. Kuth/Ranieri's Iann/Stolz scheme is such an instance of architectural concision, a lithe response to the context of a small site—a narrow alleyway behind an existing house.

And God is still in the details. All the work here is very elegantly wrought, providing a powerful critique of the architecture of virtuality and pure image that so dominates our media. Careful detailing abstracts historic tradition to a new architectural idiom while retaining a sense of indigenous assembly. Joinery is always the moment of truth for architectures of gravity.

Various projects in this collection might equally be said to embody modernity's sense of simplicity and craft, drawing from the elegance of Quaker architecture, the austerity of New England, and the structural directness of Native American construction. Whether in the precise, artful modulation of transparency, opacity, and density in Shim-Sutcliffe Architects' Island House or in the elegance of proportion, craft, and detail in the Tower House, the firm's work manages to combine modesty with enormous refinement. Wesley Wei's Media, Pennsylvania, house extension was influenced by local craft traditions and by Mies's aesthetic, elegantly juxtaposing stone, metal sheeting, wood siding, and glass.

Today's environmental climate demands an architecture that lies lightly on the land. Understanding building in terms of its respiration, its participation in larger ecological and climatic cycles, and its contribution to local styles of self-sufficiency are some of the most pressing questions for practice today. The work here understands this via a certain reserve, a kind of unspoken sumptuary law that evokes a reticence to waste. These projects are all very much *in* the landscape, both in the sense of their visual porosity and in the idea that their architectural form enhances its circumstances by augmenting and understanding them, rather than by dominating or transforming them.

If the idea of local identity is bound up with geological, meteorological, political, and cultural difference, its authentic expression will be increasingly modulated by art. The eight practices in this book are heirs to the research of their predecessors on the land but are also pioneers, adjusting to the challenge of the overlapping virtual regions in which we all dwell and to the precision with which the afflicted earth demands architects respond to it. All the firms assert that, given the waning relevance of the literal continuation of traditional building practices, the invigoration of artistic differences is a crucial road for the recovery of a meaningful sense of particularity in place.

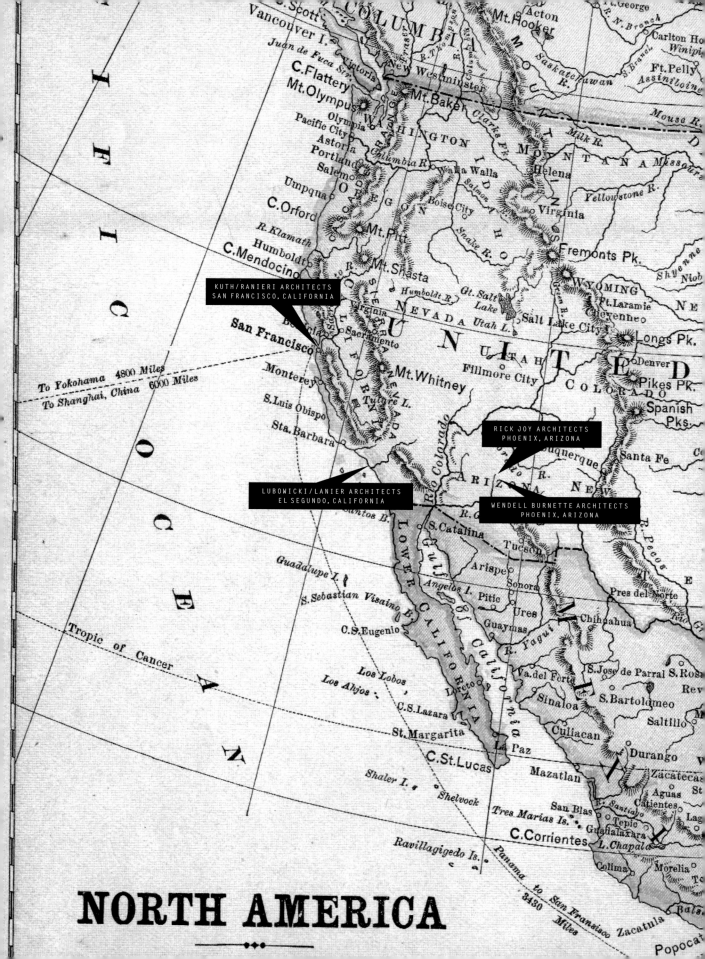

KUTH/RANIERI ARCHITECTS
SAN FRANCISCO, CALIFORNIA

RICK JOY ARCHITECTS
PHOENIX, ARIZONA

LUBOWICKI/LANIER ARCHITECTS
EL SEGUNDO, CALIFORNIA

WENDELL BURNETTE ARCHITECTS
PHOENIX, ARIZONA

NORTH AMERICA

BRIAN MACKAY-LYONS
ARCHITECTURE URBAN DESIGN
HALIFAX, NOVA SCOTIA

SHIM-SUTCLIFFE ARCHITECTS
TORONTO, ONTARIO

SHoP:
SHARPLES HOLDEN PASQUARELLI
NEW YORK, NEW YORK

WESLEY WEI ARCHITECTS
PHILADELPHIA, PENNSYLVANIA

Shim-Sutcliffe Architects

Island House

This summer house functions both as its own landscape and as an integral part of the existing landscape. The clients, a couple in their fifties with a passion for sailing, chose as the site a rural island in the St. Lawrence River dotted with dairy farms. Shim-Sutcliffe Architects was intrigued with the challenge of designing an island within an island in this agrarian context.

All that is visible on the approach to the house, via a rural road, is a long, low concrete wall set into a gentle slope. The St. Lawrence River is discernible in the distance. From the road, the entry to the house is a path between two gentle berms. These sculpted clover-covered mounds obscure the roadway from the house, establishing visual continuity between the surrounding meadow and the adjacent farmland.

Two rectilinear volumes with flat rooftops and a taller, horizontally striated structure gradually rise into view—low, rectilinear planes interlocking around a taller, cubic space. Both of the flat rooftops are planted with wildflowers and blend into the meadow. The taller edifice, a double-height living room, is set in a man-made reflecting pool planted with rushes—the most obvious manifestation of the architects' island-within-an-island theme.

The landscape design reinforces the wild as well as the agricultural and pastoral qualities of the island environment. Ornamental grasses set against natural field grasses and wildflowers such as catnip, yarrow, and clover form the landscape palette, while water lilies and bulrushes grow in the rectilinear pond. A crushed rock "dry garden," delineated by an extended retaining wall along the edge of the grounds, contains large slabs of limestone that were excavated from the site.

The western, public block contains indoor and outdoor dining and a kitchen. The eastern, private wing contains a master bedroom, bathroom, study, and storage. Within the eastern portion of the house, a volume containing a bathroom and dressing room forms a freestanding island. The thick north wall contains storage, stairway to the basement level, and bathroom. The entry looks down through the upper portion of the living room pavilion across a meadow to the river beyond. A freestanding fireplace acts as a pivotal point between living, dining, and entry.

CREDITS

Project
Island House,
St. Lawrence River,
Ontario, 2002

Client
Kevin and Carol Reilly

Architect
Shim-Sutcliffe Architects:
Brigitte Shim, Howard
Sutcliffe, Donald Chong,
Jason Emery Groen,
John O'Connor

Structural Engineer
Blackwell Engineering

Mechanical Engineer
Toews Engineering

Builder
Peabody and
Sheedy Construction

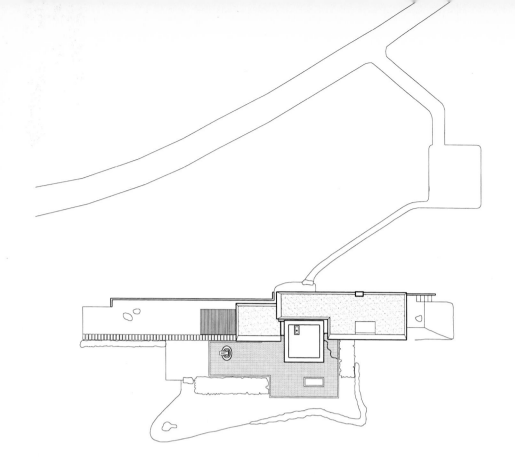

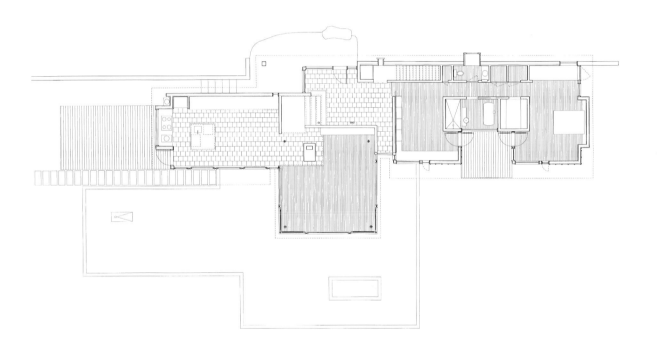

Tower House and Restaurant Renovation

An unusual hybrid, this urban project connects an existing renovated restaurant to a new townhouse. Rundles is one of southern Ontario's finest restaurants and was founded in a reconfigured boathouse along the Avon River. The new attached residence, built for the owner of Rundles, sits on a sixteen-by-forty-three-foot lot. The extremely narrow site, formerly a small parking lot, forced the architects to build vertically rather than horizontally in order to accommodate a living room, dining room, master bedroom, bathroom, kitchen, and study.

The three-story house is organized around a small wood-framed light court, a circulation core that connects each room and floor level. The floors and ceilings of the living space split and shift vertically, dividing the north and south portions of the house and emphasizing the very different characters of the front and back of the site. The north face, with the entrance to both house and restaurant, sits on a well-trafficked small-city strip dominated by apartment buildings; the back of the lot opens southward to pastoral vistas of the river. The view from the house flips from the urban lane to the river according to floor level.

The alterations to Rundles included a new entry and entrance ramp, a bay window at the front of the building, and the reworking of the two dining rooms. Every October, at the end of Stratford's busy tourist season (which revolves around the nearby Shakespeare Theatre), Rundles transforms into a chef's school, requiring the two dining rooms to be very flexible.

On the exterior, the interdependence of restaurant and residence is both reinforced and denied by the shared front facade—a monolithic wall of light-washed concrete. Once again playing on the vertical and the horizontal, the architects designed the restaurant facade as a landscape plane and the tower front as a vast portrait plane. On the interior, the house and restaurant share an angled party wall that is perpendicular to the front facade. The entry to Rundles is along this concrete wall, which also frames a small garden to the north and a water court to the south. The powerful simplicity of form on the exterior belies the multilevel spatial complexities of the building's interior.

CREDITS

Project
Tower House and
Restaurant Renovation,
Stratford, Ontario, 2002

Client
James Morris

Architect
Shim-Sutcliffe Architects:
Brigitte Shim, Howard
Sutcliffe, Donald Chong,
Jason Emery Groen,
John O'Connor

Structural Engineer
Blackwell Engineering

Mechanical Engineer
Toews Engineering

Builder
Dan Paul Design Build

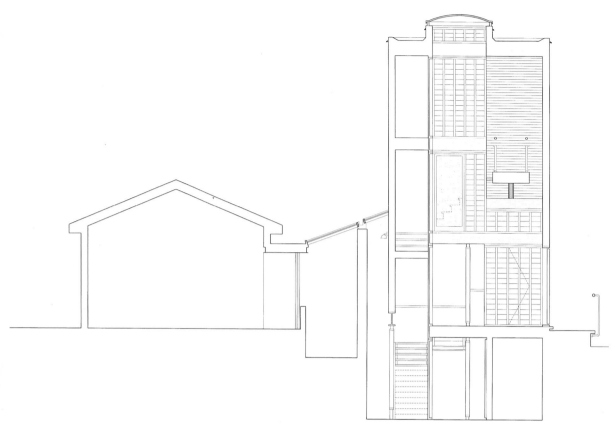

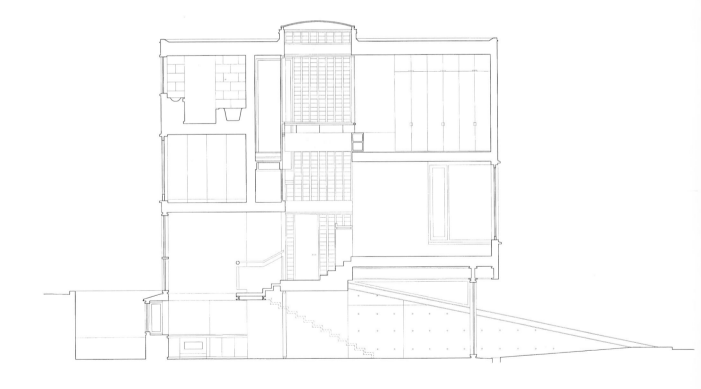

Brian

MacKay-Lyons

Architecture

Urban Design

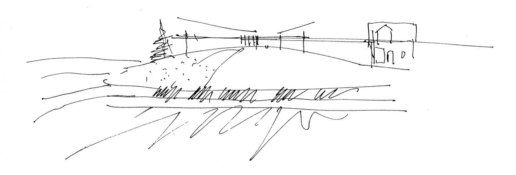

Howard House

This long, two-story shed in Halifax is home to a young family of four. Bedrooms, a double-height living room, a kitchen, and a garage are strung along the thirteen-foot-wide building. A skylit void cuts through the rear of the house, providing cross ventilation during the summer and a year-round visual connection to the surrounding land. The rest of the house is focused on the waterfront location, capturing spectacular views of Fawson Cove Bay.

Materials and construction methods were borrowed from the local boat-building industry: corrugated steel, metal and wood siding, galvanized-steel roofing, visible open trusses, and cable and turnbuckle assemblies are unexpected but ready-made solutions to the area's harsh weather conditions. A cast-concrete element containing a stairway and fireplace is placed on the west side of the building to break prevailing winds. The windows on the opposite, east side are bigger to allow summer heat gain.

CREDITS

Project
Howard House,
West Pennant,
Nova Scotia, 1998

Client
Vivian and David Howard

Architect
Brian MacKay-Lyons
Architecture Urban Design:
Brian MacKay-Lyons,
Niall Savage, Trevor
Davies, Talbot Sweetapple

Structural Engineer
Campbell Comeau
Engineering Ltd.

Builder
Andrew Watts

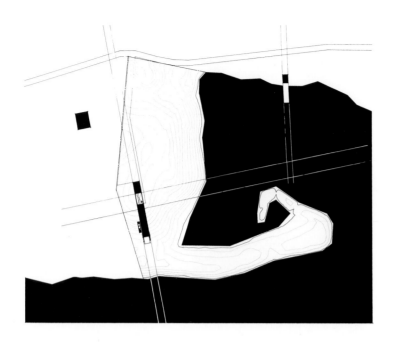

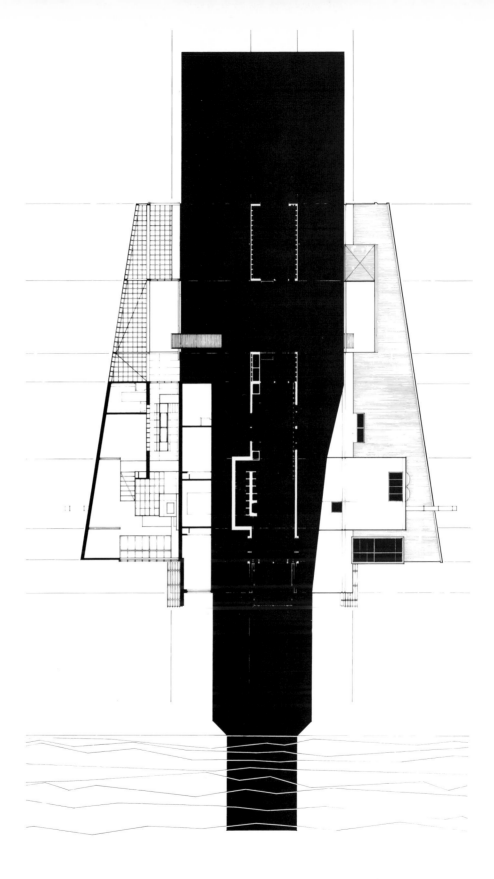

1. RIVER PUBLIC

PRIVATE

2. POND

3. POND

PUBLIC

4. SEA

House #22

House #22 sits dramatically exposed atop a glacial hill overlooking the Atlantic Ocean. The site offers ocean views to the south, east, and west and the romantic vista of a local fishing village to the north. The project exploits a simple parti to rather powerful effect: two cube-shaped buildings, one large and one small, are connected along a north-south axis.

Both cubes—main house and freestanding guest quarters—have extensive glazing, corrugated metal, concrete block, and hemlock siding wrapped around wood frames. Jumbo scupper drains are important visual elements, cantilevering out from the roof of each cube. The timber framing is visible on the interior of the buildings: hemlock trusses dominate the second-floor master bedroom and float above the double-height living room.

CREDITS

Project
House #22, Lower LaHave,
Nova Scotia, 1998

Architect
Brian MacKay-Lyons
Architecture Urban Design:
Brian MacKay-Lyons,
Bruno Weber, Rob Meyer,
Marc Cormier

Structural Engineer
Campbell Comeau
Engineering Ltd.

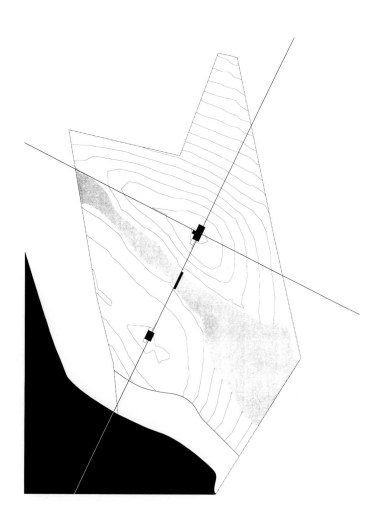

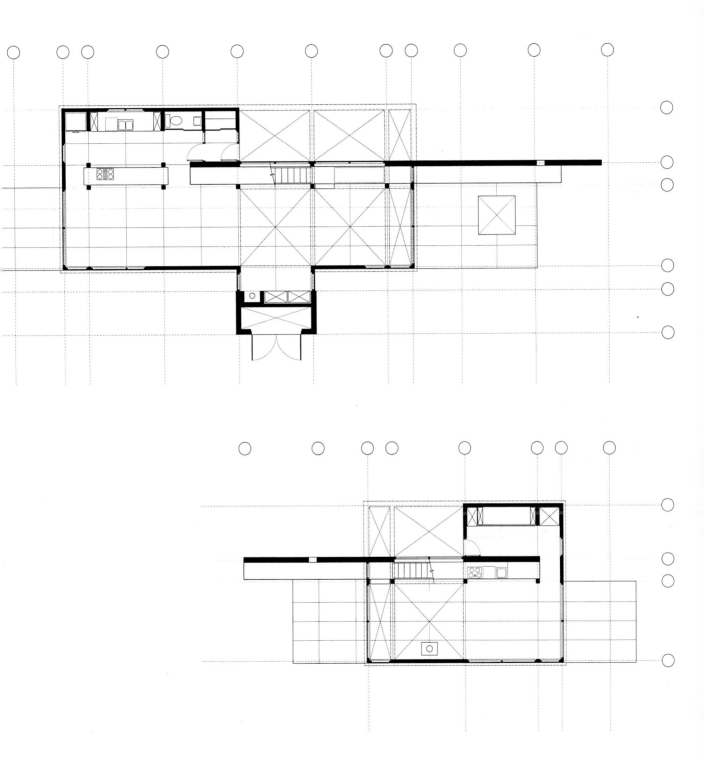

Danielson Cottage

This project, programmatically and physically similar to House #22 but on a smaller scale and budget, perches on a hill formed by glaciers on the northern edge of Nova Scotia in Cape Breton. Also a pair of wooden cubes connected on a north-south axis, this design is a residence for two with a separate guest house. Both volumes have basic interiors. The large cube is mostly uninsulated and constructed of two-by-ten timbers capped by an aluminum and steel roof. Like an enormous candy wrapper, this roof folds up and over, enveloping the house and sheltering the structure from the winds. Corrugated plastic both conceals and reveals rafters and trusses where the roof does not descend over the building. On the inside, sliding timber panels separate the heated areas from those without insulation.

CREDITS

Project
Danielson Cottage,
Smelt Brook,
Nova Scotia, 1998

Client
Esther and Bill Danielson

Architect
Brian MacKay-Lyons
Architecture Urban Design:
Brian MacKay-Lyons,
Bruno Weber, Trevor
Davies, Darryl Jones

Structural Engineer
Campbell Comeau
Engineering Ltd.

Builder
Andrew Watts

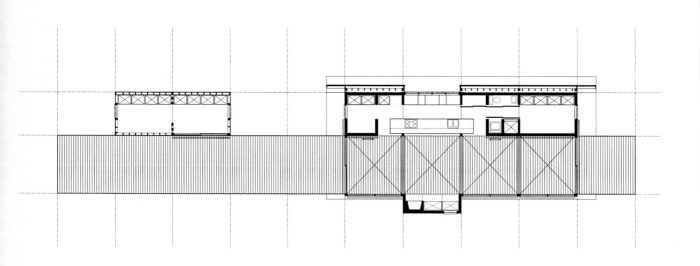

Rick Joy

Architects

Tubac House

This one-bedroom house and connected guest house were inspired by the form of a geode: a rough exterior disguises a jewel-like interior. Rugged structural wood-frame shells clad in twenty-four-gauge custom-weathered steel characterize the exterior; the interior is transformed with clean white plaster, translucent glass, stainless steel, maple, and elegant detailing. The house is topped with a combination of rusted corrugated steel and one-quarter-inch plate-steel sloped roofing, creating an object in the landscape that blends marvelously into the surrounding red desert.

In order to maximize views of the dramatic landscape, Rick Joy Architects inserted the house into a shelf cut into a hill and demarcated by two U-shaped seven-foot-high concrete retaining walls. The clients, a retired astronomer and his wife, chose the south-facing four-acre site for its incomparable celestial viewing and for its vistas to the Tumacacaori mountain peak, the San Cayetano mountains, and the expansive desert panorama. Fifty miles south of Tucson and fifteen miles from the Mexican border, the area is famous for its clear, star-saturated night skies and frequent electrical storms. The Smithsonian Institution's Fred Lawrence Whipple Observatory is visible in the distance.

Included in the four-thousand-square-foot project are two studies, an optical telescope platform, a garage, and a large courtyard, all on one level. A cast concrete stair leads to the sophisticated, shaded courtyard, which beautifully blurs the usual sharp edge between inside and outside. The courtyard is defined by foliage, large rectilinear planters, and pools of various sizes, including a black granite negative-edge cube reminiscent of the work of artist Donald Judd. The house exterior appears as two colliding rectilinear sheds animated inside and out by elevated and protruding rectangular steel-box penetrations. These volumetric elements cleverly encase the vast expanses of glazing that serve as windows for the house. The lowest and most protuberant box is the main entry vestibule.

CREDITS

Project
Tubac House,
Tubac, Arizona, 2001

Architect
Rick Joy Architects:
Rick Joy, Andy Tinucci,
Franz Buhler

Structural Engineer
Southwest Structural
Engineers, Inc.

Mechanical/Plumbing
Otterbein Engineering

Landscape
Michael Boucher
Landscape Architect

Builder
Rick Joy Architects

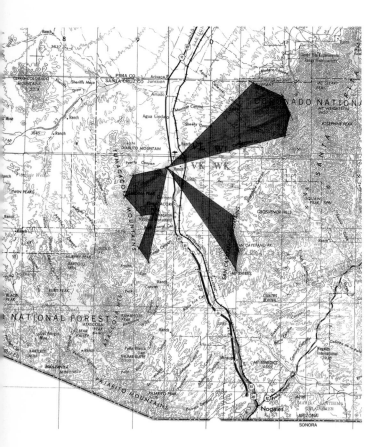

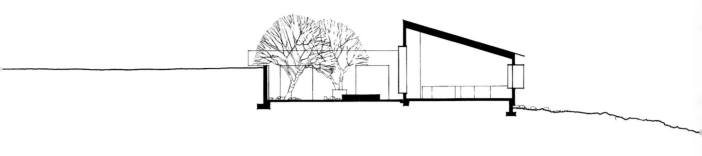

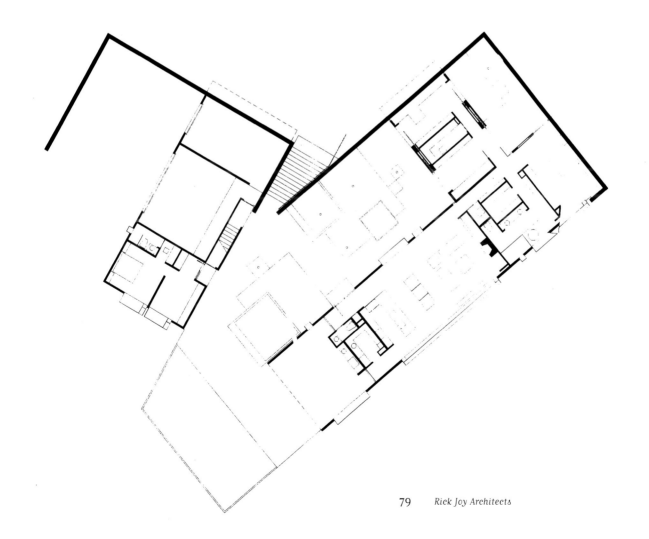

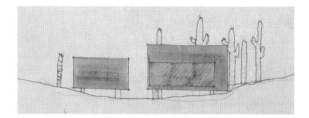

Casa Jax

This fifteen-hundred-square-foot winter retreat commissioned by a California-based "snowbird" rests in a secluded, low-lying corner of the Tucson Mountain foothills. Nestled into a naturally formed solid-granite bowl, the house sits on the edge of the Saguaro National Forest and is surrounded by lush vegetation: ocotillo, barrel, prickly pear, and ancient twenty-five-foot-high saguaro cacti. The architects divided the house into three separate rectilinear buildings, each containing a different program. The largest structure houses the living room and dining and kitchen space; the medium element houses the bedroom; the smallest building is the den/guest room. Each steel-frame, steel-plate-clad pod is elevated on reinforced-concrete piers and covered by a flat, plantation-teak roof. There are no formal walkways connecting the buildings; they are linked only by a desert path, creating the illusion that the structures were simply dropped from the sky.

The siting of the boxlike volumes was driven by the architects' temporal notion of the desert's "perfect view." Each interior was designed around a precise viewpoint at a particular time of day, resulting in selective window placement and making the house function much like a clock. The focal point of the living cube is the spectacular drama of the sun setting over the mountains and the rising lights of Tucson's nightscape. The bedroom faces the morning sun: as it emerges over the Tucson Mountains, it backlights the saguaros and ocotillo in the foreground. The guest suite has a more introspective stance, looking out on cacti and local rock outcroppings.

CREDITS

Project
Casa Jax,
Tucson, Arizona, 2002

Architect
Rick Joy Architects:
Rick Joy, Andy Tinucci,
Chelsea Grassinger

Structural Engineer
Southwest Structural
Engineers, Inc.

Mechanical/Plumbing
Otterbein Engineering

Builder
Rick Joy Architects

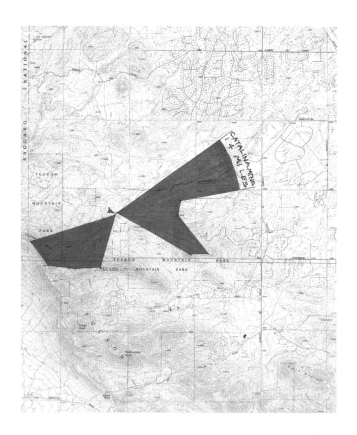

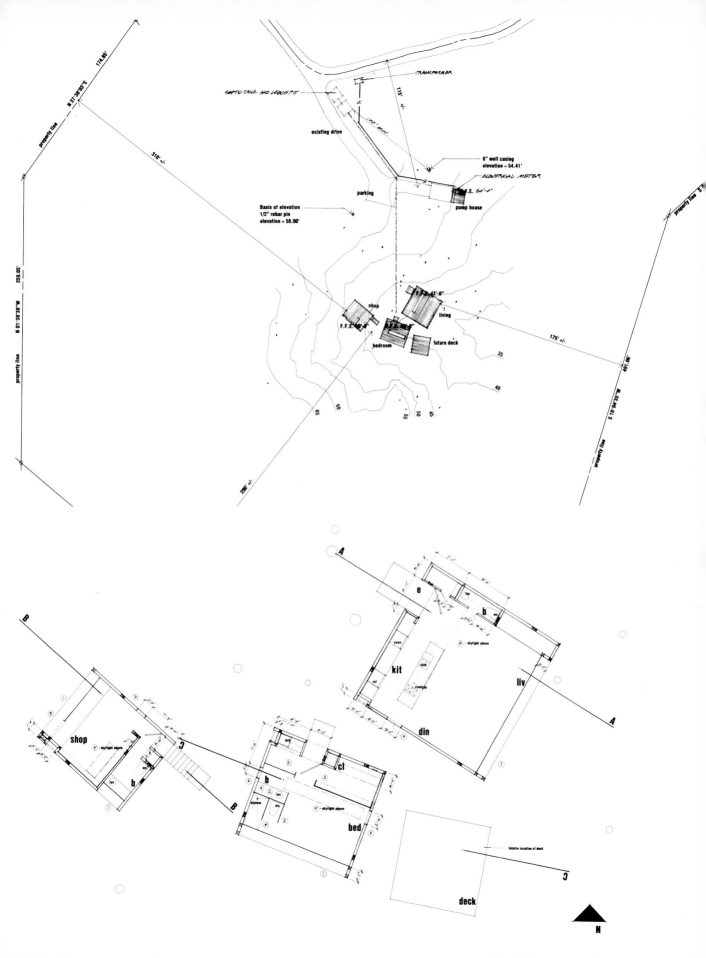

TRANSFORMER

SEPTIC TANK AND LEACH PIT

existing drive

6" well casing
elevation = 54.41'

ELECTRICAL METER

F.F.E. 60'-0"

pump house

parking

Basis of elevation
1/2" rebar pin
elevation = 58.00'

F.F.E. 43'-0"

living

shop

F.F.E. 46'-0"

F.F.E. 46'-0"

bedroom

future deck

property line
N 37°36'03"E
174.65'

property line
N 01°38'38"W
259.05'

property line

310' +/-

290' +/-

65

60

55

50

45

40

35

175' +/-

property line
S 18°04'35"W
491.06'

property line

A

e

b

kit

sink

oven

ref

cooktop

skylight above

liv

din

B

shop

skylight above

lav

b

C

b

cl

lav

lav

shower

wc

skylight above

bed

B

future location of deck

C

deck

N

Wendell Burnette Architects

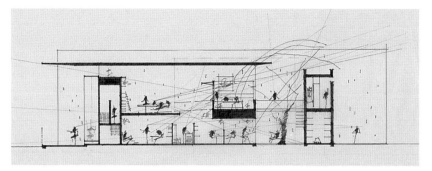

Studio for David Michael Miller Associates

Mature mesquite trees on the downtown Scottsdale site informed the plan for this interior designer's studio. Wendell Burnette Architects planned a narrow, twenty-by-ninety-foot building to accommodate the prized flora. A private courtyard toward the back of the twenty-five-foot-high structure envelops the largest tree, which peeks out over the building from both front and back. A wooded garden lines the building's east side.

The architects did not cram the building between the street and the parking lot. Inspired by a free local commodity—sunshine—and in keeping with vernacular walled architecture, common throughout the Southwest, the designers developed the building as a sandwich: two monolithic walls contain a creamy daylight filling. The studio resembles a freestanding office building in a small garden rather than a typical maximum-square-footage urban structure.

The studio's western wall is solid concrete block; the eastern wall, also concrete block, is punctured with playful cutouts that bring strips of horizontal and vertical light into the interior. The two ends of the building are vast expanses of glass. The south side, a double-height, glazed facade, is an intriguing storefront—free advertising for the client. An extended steel canopy shades a granite bench and a tiny plaza in front of the studio. The northern facade, also double-height, looks out over the private courtyard. Even the required city dumpster is discreetly encased in concrete block and a large mill-finished stainless-steel gate. The studio interior, a collaboration between architect and client, consists of a reception area, kitchen/workroom, and two workstations on the first floor and a conference room/library and office on the upper floor.

CREDITS

Project
Studio for David Michael Miller Associates, Scottsdale, Arizona, 1999

Client
David Michael Miller

Architect
Wendell Burnette Architects: Wendell Burnette, Michael Le Blanc, Christopher Alt

Interior Design
David Michael Miller Associates

Structural Engineer
Rudow and Berry Inc.

Mechanical Engineer
Technica, Inc.

Landscape Design
Ten Eyck Landscape Architects

General Contractor
Construction Zone

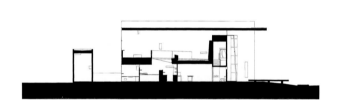

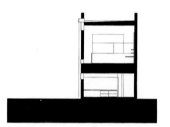

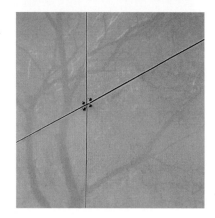

Tocker Residence

Wendell Burnette Architects was commissioned by a young couple to design a house that would be an oasis—despite the busy road next to the site. To achieve such an atmosphere, the two-thousand-square-foot house was placed in the northwest corner of the half-acre lot and raised up one story. The site, a volcanic mountain ridge known locally as the Echo Mountain foothills, offered a considerable slope and spectacular views.

Designed on a tight budget—under two hundred dollars per square foot—all living space was enclosed in a single economical structure. The timber-framed volume, supported on charcoal-masonry walls in a lateral-pinwheel brace, contains the living room, bedroom, kitchen, and bathroom. A ground-level open-topped pool house at the edge of the slope anchors the main volume to the site. The effect is that of a floating living space, a box of light, connected to a body of water that appears to melt into the horizon. Both structures face a dramatic vista of the downtown Phoenix skyline stacked up against South Mountain and the Sierra Estrella range.

CREDITS

Project
Tocker Residence,
Phoenix, Arizona, 2002

Client
Brad Tocker

Architect
Wendell Burnette
Architects:
Wendell Burnette,
Christopher Alt

Structural Engineer
Rudow and Berry, Inc.

Mechanical Engineer
Otterbein Engineering

Landscape Design
Debra Burnette
Landscape Design

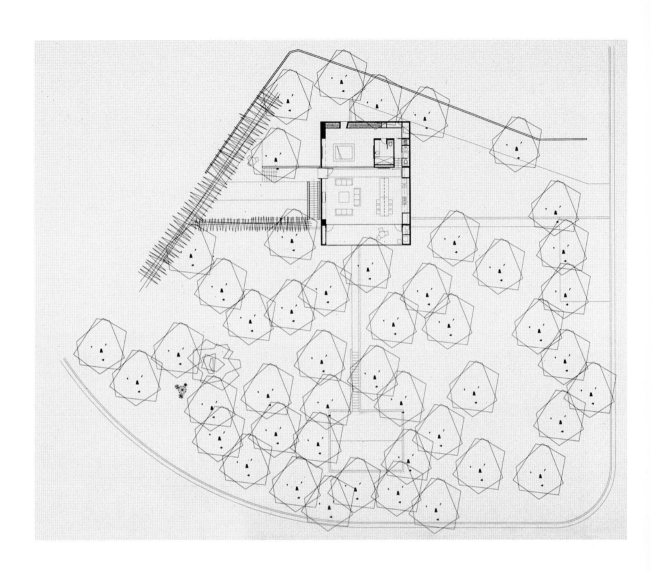

PHILADELPHIA, PENNSYLVANIA

Wesley Wei

Architects

Easton Guest House

This project is located on thirty-five wooded acres on the Eastern Shore of Maryland. Built as a second residence on the property, the guest house complements a 5,500-square-foot main house and is intended to accommodate the owner's adult children, grandchildren, and guests. Wesley Wei Architects played with the allocation of the standard domestic program of the house—living room, dining room, kitchen, baths, bedrooms, and storage—to maximize views of the Tred Avon River, flipping a traditional residential layout into what the firm describes as an "upside-down house." The private realm is unexpectedly located on the ground floor, while expansive living and entertaining space is located upstairs, affording views of the garden and river. A lead-coated copper roof and strategically placed stucco cladding block the view into the building from the main house and swimming pool.

Throughout the house the architects have imparted a sense of ambiguity to conventional architectural elements by cleverly manipulating them. For example, the masonry walls that define the boundaries of the house extend beyond the house, becoming dramatic sculptures in the landscape. The entryway is formed by the juncture of two perpendicular brick walls. On the interior, the main vertical circulation route, a set of maple stairs, transforms into a dining table projected from the stairway into the dining area.

CREDITS

Project
Easton Guest House,
Easton, Maryland, 2000

Architect
Wesley Wei Architects:
Wesley Wei, Daniel Magno,
Catherine Tighe, Andrew
Philips, Douglas Patt,
Suzanne Brandt

General Contractor
Ned Orme

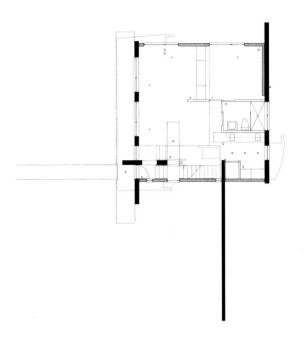

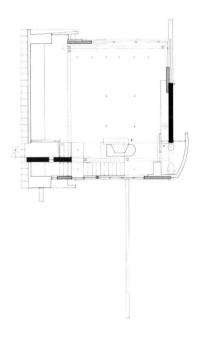

Media Residence

This renovation and addition to a late-eighteenth-century farmhouse twenty miles southwest of Philadelphia was defined by both the client's attitude toward his collection of contemporary art and his desire for privacy. The architects removed older, awkward additions to the original two-story, seven-hundred-square-foot schist and fieldstone farmhouse, then built a 2,500-square-foot extension apportioned asymmetrically on either side of the remaining structure. The exterior of the house, both front and back, now appears as a dramatic, volumetric collage. The innovative choice of materials—Cor-Ten steel, lead-coated copper, and poured concrete—contrasts vividly with the thick masonry walls of the farmhouse. The old and the new are integrated on the interior by a clear pathway. This cut connects the small kitchen (the client almost never cooks) and an outdoor pond filled with exotic koi.

The ground level is an eighteen-foot-high loftlike gallery, built to house an enormous Anselm Kiefer canvas, and sitting spaces. The master bedroom floats over this gallery on a steel frame. The gallery, which also includes pieces by Georg Baselitz, Francesco Clemente, Alberto Giacometti, Louise Nevelson, and others, is fully visible from the site's bucolic setting, while the upper-level sleeping area is veiled by a theatrical lead-coated copper "mask."

CREDITS

Project
Media Residence, Media, Pennsylvania, 2000

Architect
Wesley Wei Architects: Wesley Wei, Stephen Mileto, Caitlin Moore, Joel Zeigler, Taylor Lawson

Interior Designer
Maria Izak Nevelson Interior Design

General Contractor
Phillip Johnson Construction, Inc.

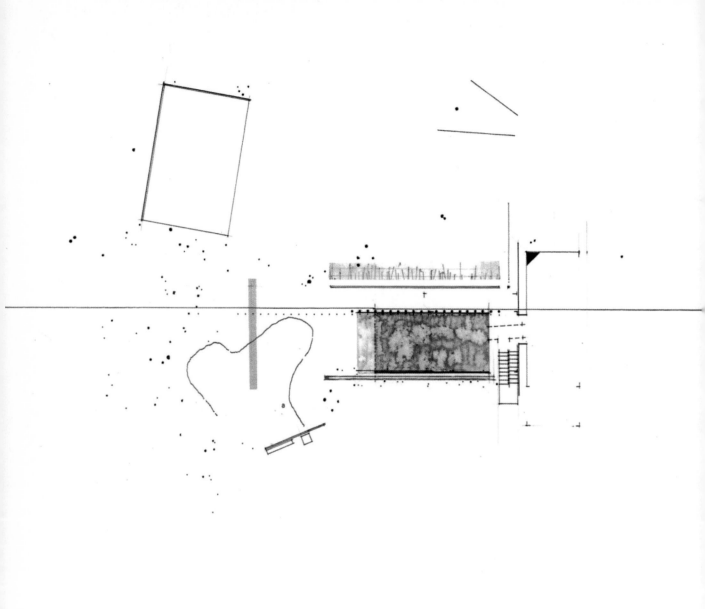

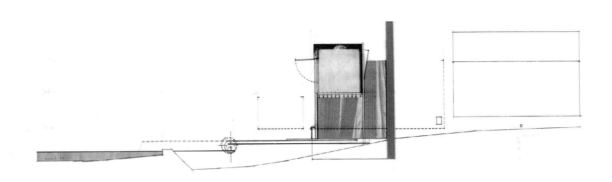

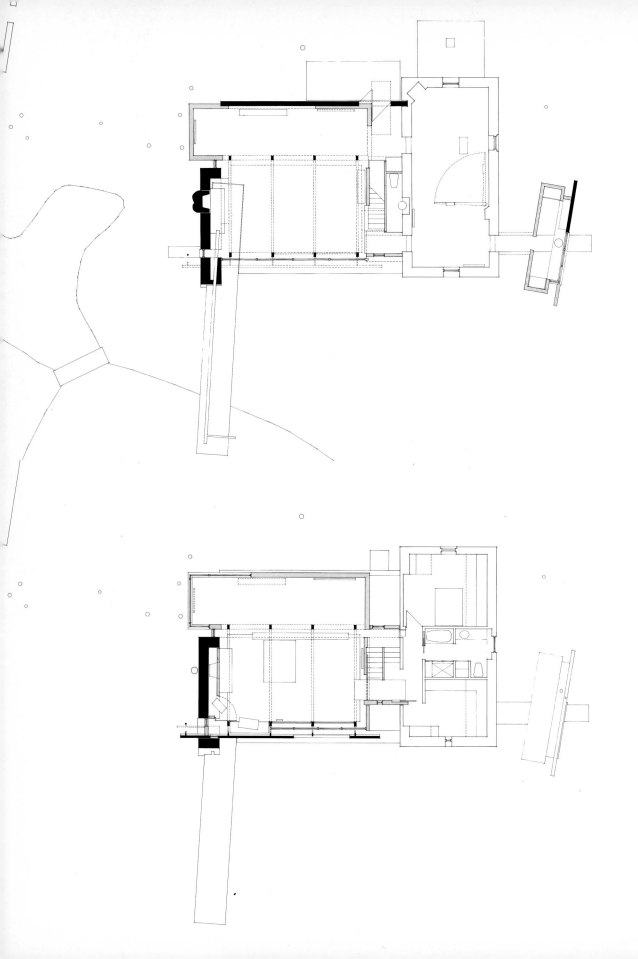

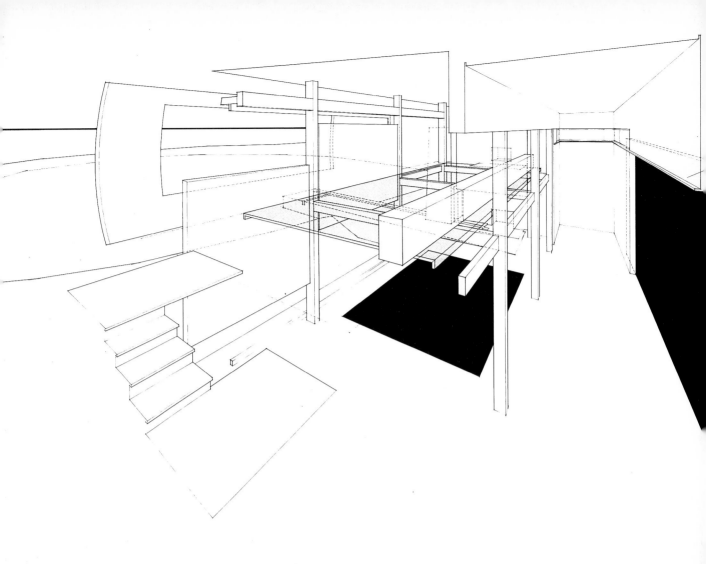

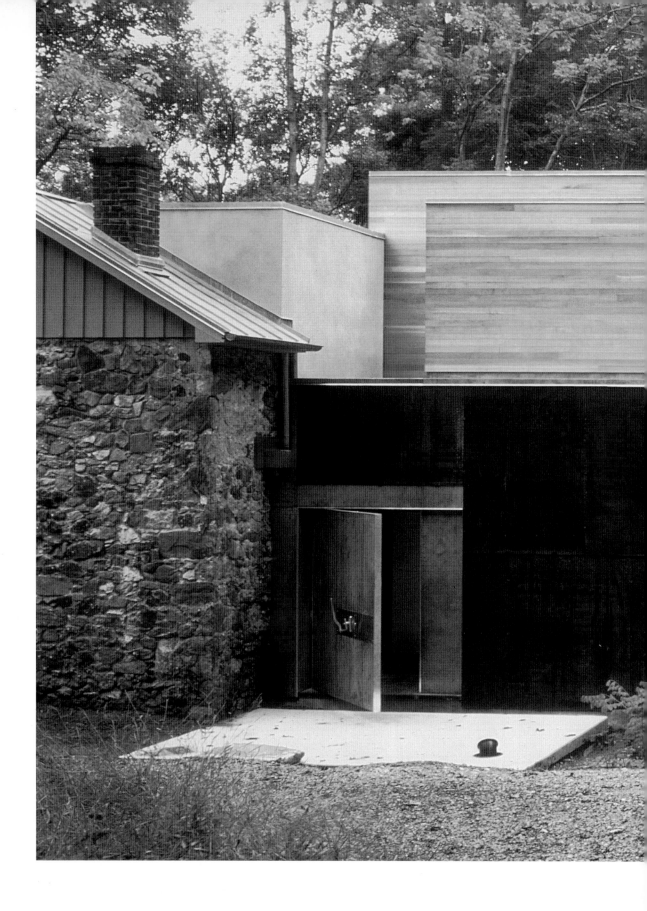

Philadelphia Chinatown Community Center

Commissioned by the Philadelphia Chinatown Development Corporation, this unbuilt thirty-five-thousand-square-foot facility was intended to be a growth catalyst for the local neighborhood. The design accommodates various activities while serving as a visible icon for the local Chinese community. Wesley Wei Architects proposed locating the building across the Vine Street Expressway from the current edge of Chinatown, transforming the visual and social center of the area. The theoretical analysis presented to the community by the architects describes the building as analogous to parts of human anatomy. The front of the building, which extends above and beyond the rest of the edifice, represents the center's "head." This literal brain contains large meeting rooms on the second and third floors that survey Chinatown to the south. The "body" of the building houses a gallery, library stacks, carrels, and workrooms. The entire program is held together by "ribs": the structural framework of the centrally located recreation and meeting hall that extends out from and interweaves with the main piers that support the building.

CREDITS

Project
Philadelphia Chinatown
Community Center,
Philadelphia,
Pennsylvania, 1998
(unbuilt)

Architect
Wesley Wei Architects:
Wesley Wei, Andrew
Philips, Douglas Pratt,
Cary Paik

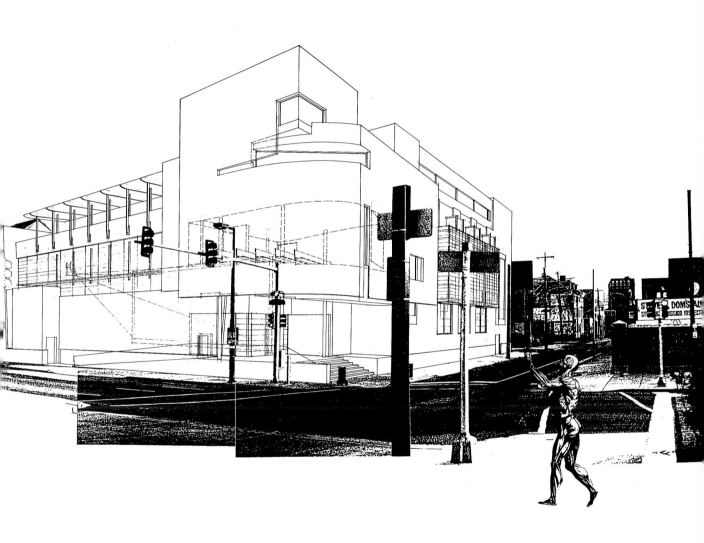

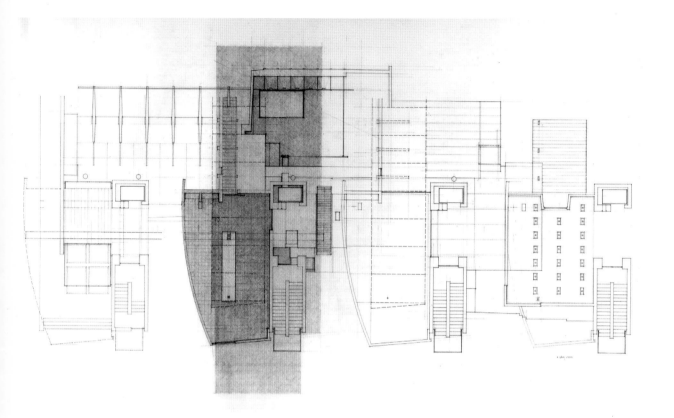

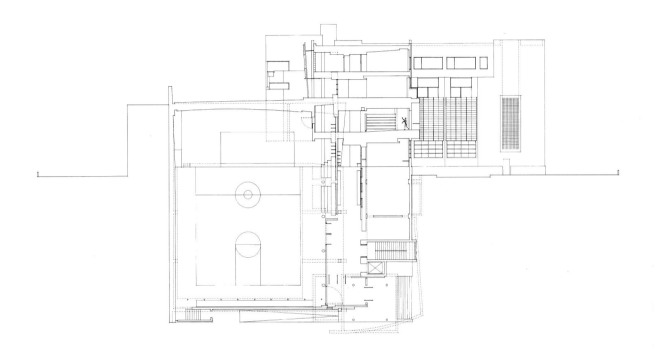

EAST

SHoP:

Sharples

Holden

Pasquarelli

Mitchell Park

An unusual public-private enterprise, Mitchell Park is one element of a major three-and-a-half-acre waterfront revitalization along Greenport Harbor. Commissioned by the village of Greenport, Long Island, the seven-year project has involved a broad partnership of individuals, businesses, organizations, and government.

The design accomplishes two goals: it creates a pleasing landscape and it links surrounding landmarks, notably the nearby ferry terminal and rail station. A new timber boardwalk, or harbor walk, follows the curve of the shoreline and defines the boundaries of the Jerry McCarthy Amphitheater (named for a longtime Greenport bandleader), an ample village green, and a steel and glass pavilion housing an antique carousel. The amphitheater's terraced seating and low semicircular flagstone walls face Peconic Bay. A municipal marina and skating rink are planned as the next phase of the project.

CREDITS

Project
Mitchell Park, Greenport,
New York, Phase I, 2001

Client
Village of Greenport

Architect
SHoP: Sharples Holden
Pasquarelli: Christopher
Sharples, William Sharples,
Coren Sharples, Kim
Holden, Gregg Pasquarelli,
Shigeru Kuwahara, Max
Strang, Leo Chang

Structural Engineers
FTL/Happold

Mechanical Engineer
Laszlo Bodak Engineer, P.C.

Landscape Consultant
Quennell Rothschild +
Partners, LLP

Lighting Consultant
Universe Lighting

General Contractor
Carriage Hill Associates, Inc.

variegated fronts

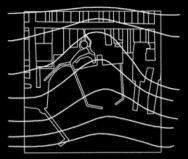

boater

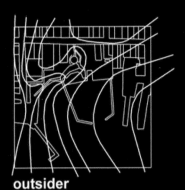

outsider

villager

shopper

vectors

harbor

marina

main street

wharf

basins

floods

tides

events

fields

SHoP: Sharples Holden Pasquarelli

145

Light Bridges

This proposed development comprises two residential towers, below-grade parking, and ground-level retail. The project is located in the Brooklyn district known as DUMBO—"Down Under the Manhattan Bridge Overpass." Gentrification is currently occurring in DUMBO, an industrial neighborhood dominated by nineteenth- and twentieth-century brick factories near the Navy Yard, a designated historic district, and the already posh Brooklyn Heights.

Light Bridges is named for its design: a glass-enclosed bridge connects the two towers. The forms of both bridge and buildings are based on computer modeling that helped the architects maximize light and optimize views of Manhattan. The massing of the building alters as it rises, shifting from an industrial base to thinner, sleeker residential units.

CREDITS

Project
Light Bridges at Jay Street, Brooklyn, New York, 2000–

Client
Jeffrey M. Brown & Associates

Architect
SHoP: Sharples Holden Pasquarelli: Christopher Sharples, William Sharples, Coren Sharples, Kim Holden, Gregg Pasquarelli, Richard Garber, Johnathon Malie, Kris Lawson, Brandi Henderson

Structural Engineer
Buro Happold

MEP Engineers
Buro Happold

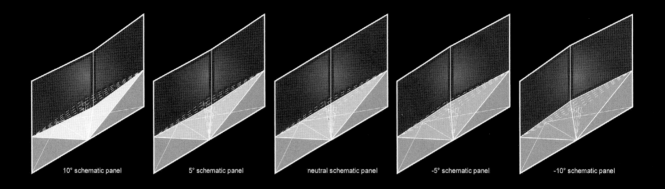

| 10° schematic panel | 5° schematic panel | neutral schematic panel | -5° schematic panel | -10° schematic panel |

Schatz geometry

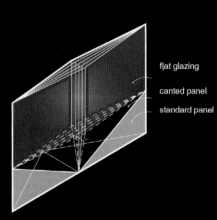

flat glazing

canted panel

standard panel

schematic bay detail

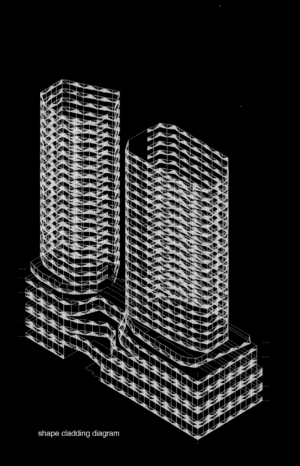

shape cladding diagram

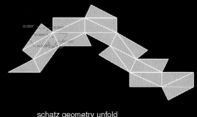

schatz geometry unfold

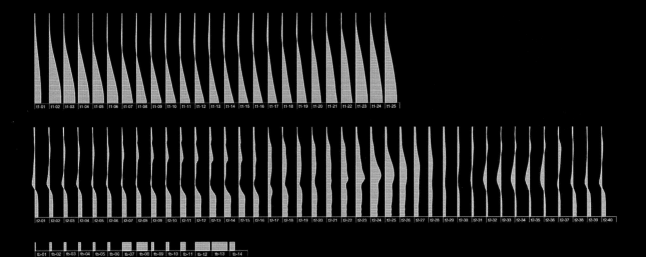

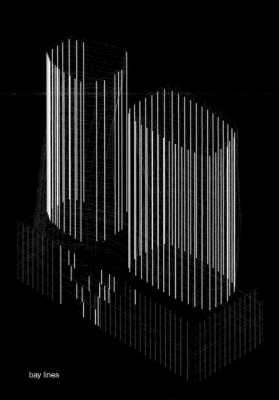

bay lines

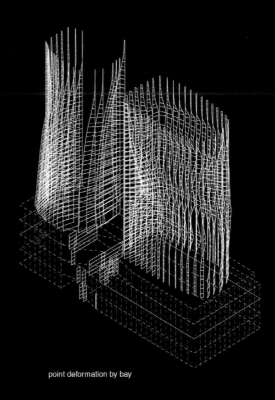

point deformation by bay

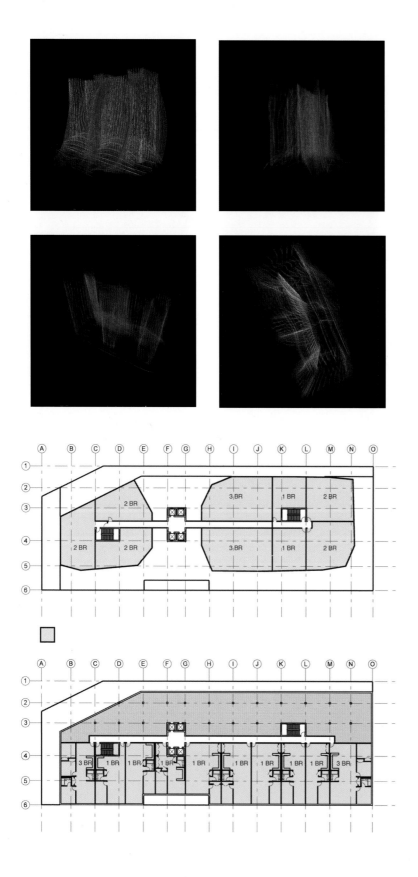

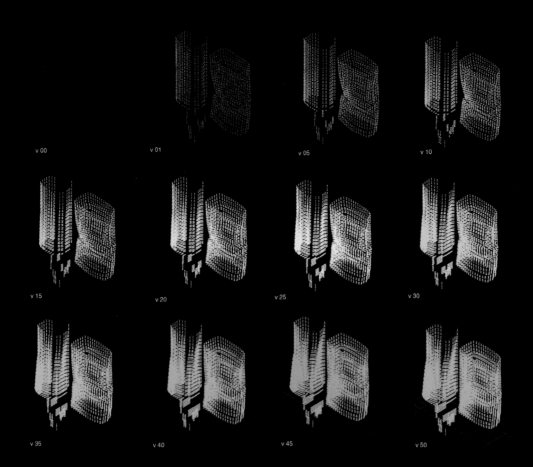

v 00   v 01   v 05   v 10

v 15   v 20   v 25   v 30

v 35   v 40   v 45   v 50

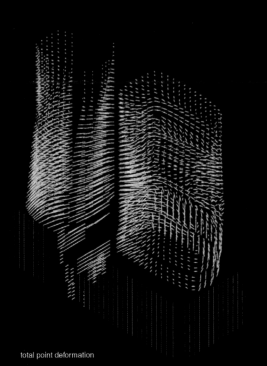

total point deformation

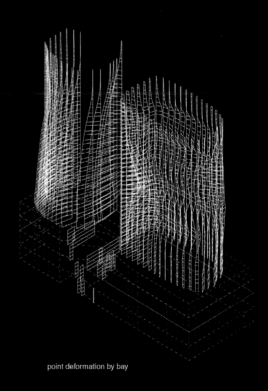

point deformation by bay

WEST

Kuth/ Ranieri Architects

Iann/Stolz Residence

This project began as a simple commission for a garage but quickly became a major renovation and expansion. A traditional wood-frame 1,800-square-foot townhouse was transformed into an open, airy, 2,500-square-foot abode surrounded by a garden. The clients, avid car aficionados, requested the installation of a three-car garage on the narrow, sloped, dead-end site. Kuth/Ranieri Architects proposed and ultimately completed extensive remodeling and reengineering that included a seismic upgrade, a full-story excavation below grade for the new garage, all-new, below-grade eight-foot foundations, new facades, and new interiors. By anchoring a series of rigid steel moment frames to an exterior "tube," the architects opened the house, providing a capacious loftlike interior and spectacular views of the Golden Gate Bridge from each of the floors.

The interior was planned entirely around the views. The central living spaces are bracketed by support zones: stairs, bathrooms, and storage. Living, dining, and kitchen areas are on the lower level; a master bedroom and guest bedroom with individual baths occupy the upper level. Contiguous flooring erases the boundary between the master bedroom and upper roof deck. Retractable shelving, sliding panels, hidden skylights, and rolling track doors offer additional flexibility. The architects chose rich but neutral materials—blackened steel, stainless steel, limestone, bleached maple, and hot-troweled plaster—to delineate the domestic program.

Elements typical of the architectural traditions of the San Francisco area—bay window, front-facing garage door, and street-side roof deck—were reinterpreted on the exterior. The street facade consists of horizontal clear-varnished mahogany panels and ledges of varying widths. This slightly undulating twenty-three-foot-wide wooden exterior is a dynamic, hybrid confection of suburban slatted garage door and local shipbuilding technology, a symbolic juxtaposition of regular and irregular systems. Toward the cornice, the wooden slats shrink in scale and the battens that divide them become closer. The meticulously well-crafted facade is strong and evocative, although the architects' primary intention was to mirror vertically the horizontal condition of the site, a narrow sliver of land that changes from city grid to open-plan house to organic garden landscape.

CREDITS

Project
Iann/Stolz Residence,
San Francisco,
California, 1999

Client
Adriane Iann and
Christian Stolz

Architect
Kuth/Ranieri Architects:
Byron Kuth, Liz Ranieri,
Andrew Dunbar, Steve
Tracy, Steve Const,
Claudia Merzario, Kale
Wisnia, Joelle Colliard

Structural Engineer
Ralph Teyssier

Contractor
Paragon General
Contractors

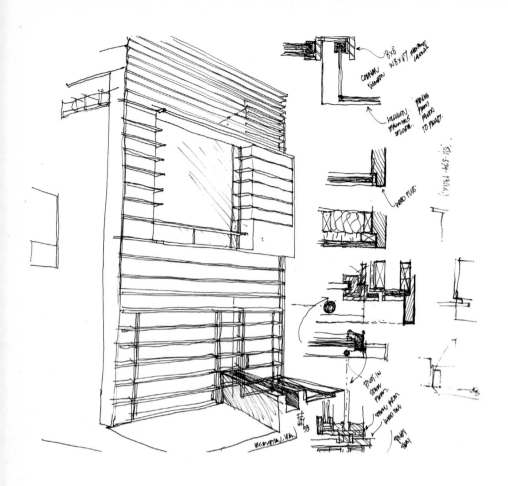

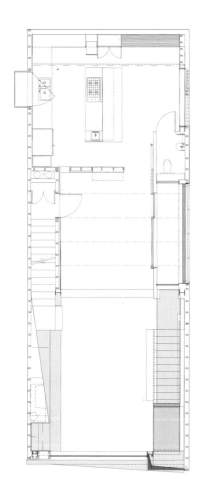
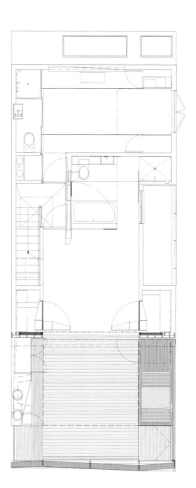

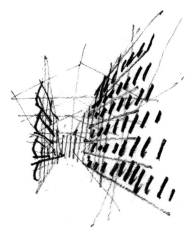

Lodi Bunkhouse

This bunkhouse, a fresh take on the vacation lodge, is in essence a souped-up, retrofitted shed. The designers converted an industrial building into a 4,200-square-foot holiday house suited to the needs of an extended family. The fluid and adaptable interior includes four bedrooms, a media room, and a series of communal spaces that can be easily reconfigured by the building's users.

The bunkhouse sits on a two-acre vineyard on Napa Valley flatlands once owned by the Southern & Pacific Railroad. Parallel to an abandoned rail line and the Napa River, the building runs from north to south alongside roadways and nearby mountain ranges. The design of the bunkhouse was an exercise in linearity. A bay was added on the south side of the existing building, and the interior was completely redesigned around an axial void cut down the center of the structure. This huge nave transforms into an outdoor canopy that connects the landscape to the north and south. Thirty-by-fifteen-foot airplane hangar doors accentuate the connection, erasing the boundaries between indoor and outdoor space.

The concrete plinth and timber-frame shell of the original building were retained for financial and practical reasons, but the roof was stripped and the interior gutted. A second exoskeletal structure and a new skin envelop the salvaged frame of the building. This exterior layer of wood and semi-opaque corrugated fiberglass fulfills seismic requirements and also houses necessary environmental systems. The thick wall contains ducts from evaporative coolers, a lacework of solar voltaic cells, and a piped solar system for heating water. The building's outermost skin, the layer of transparent fiberglass sheathing, appears animated, revealing a network of pipes and cavities in a constant state of flux.

CREDITS

Project
Lodi Bunkhouse,
St. Helena, Napa Valley,
California, 2002

Client
Lodi Partnership

Architect
Kuth/Ranieri Architects:
Byron Kuth, Liz Ranieri,
Tim Rouch, Brian
Milman, Claudia Merzario,
Andrew Dunbar

Structural Engineer
Ralph Teyssier

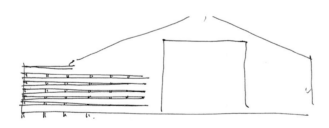

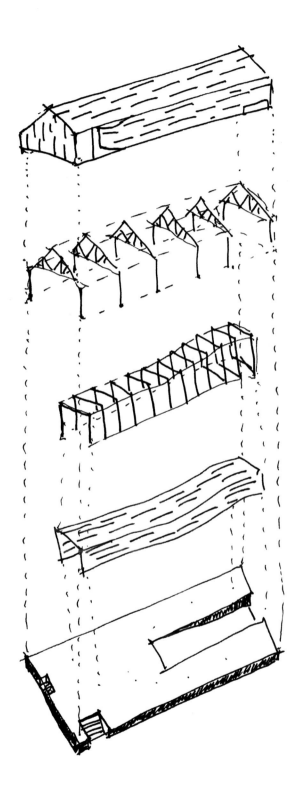

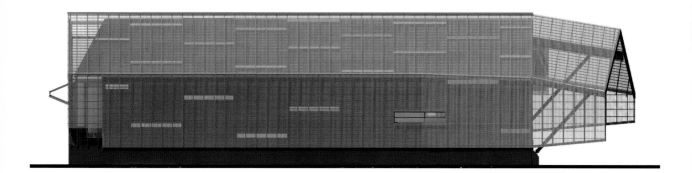

Lubowicki/ Lanier Architects

O'Neill Guest House

Lubowicki/Lanier Architects designed this camouflaged guest house to respond to its site and to an existing two-story house, an old Spanish-style bungalow several blocks north of Wilshire Boulevard. Atypical for West Los Angeles, the deep lot has a natural watercourse running through it. The site slopes twenty-six feet from the street to a pool terrace and then to the tree-lined creek. The architects took advantage of the terraced lot by building on the lowest area of the site. Service space is hidden underneath the structural metal decking system of the pool. From the main house, only the rooftop of the guest house is visible.

The architects divided the essential components of the eight-hundred-square-foot program, a living room and bedroom, into two separate architectural elements: a pair of cubes. Between the two cubes is a planter that serves as the roof for the dining area below. The two boxes, similar in size, scale, and proportion, are very different in character. The living room, a semi-open garden structure, is composed of a steel frame with horizontal copper panels, each separated by a two-inch strip of glass. These panels are mirrored by maple-plywood ones on the interior that simulate the interior of an old packing crate. The copper-clad roof is set at an angle, tilted to let in shafts of light.

The bunkerlike, stucco-clad bedroom is partially buried in the earth. Another tilted roof, this time planted with reed grasses, further disguises the structure and on the interior creates the illusion that the box is slowly opening.

CREDITS

Project
O'Neill Guest House,
West Los Angeles,
California, 1998

Client
Donna O'Neill

Architect
Lubowicki/Lanier
Architects: Susan Lanier,
Joseph Holsen,
Feliciano Reyers Jr.,
David Spinelli,
Susan Addison,
Timothy J. Williams

Structural Engineer
Parker/Resnick
Structural Engineers

Mechanical Engineer
William Comeau

Landscape Designer
Barry Campion

General Contractor
Alexander Construction &
Tony Morales Construction

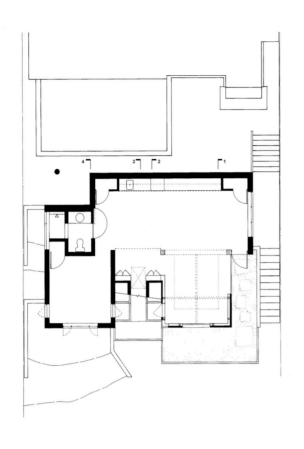

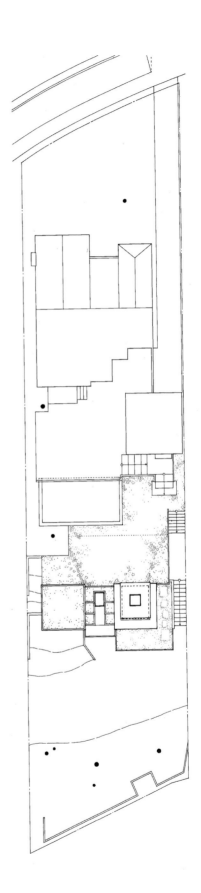

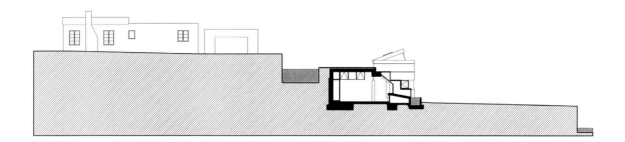

Hardy Residence

The blurring of indoor and outdoor boundaries characterizes this residential addition in a Los Angeles suburb. The site is kitty-corner to a historic house designed by R. M. Schindler; the odd juxtaposition with the existing house, a 1930s Spanish-style bungalow, was an important site consideration for the architects. Inspired by Schindler's preoccupation with the relationship between inside and outside—an exploration made especially possible by the mild local climate—the addition is centered on a large new outdoor courtyard. This garden room, dominated by two enormous eucalyptus trees, is visible and accessible from most of the house.

The addition partially envelops the old house, wrapping around it in a loose L. The kitchen and family room, joined into one large space, connect to the side of the existing house. Beyond is a transitory volume, a guest room and master bath, suspended between the inside and the outside of the existing house. A concrete-block box, this element serves as both internal and external wall. Throughout the project, program is also reflected in the building's materials, a minimal palette of stucco, copper, and concrete block. A glass-and-wood clerestory above the master-bath shower unit plays on both material and scale, further defining each unit as separate but connected entities. The master bedroom completes the L plan with a private rear courtyard. Adding to the project's introverted character are the windows on the new portion of the house: set quite high, they let in light but do not allow for a view in or out.

CREDITS

Project
Hardy Residence,
Los Angeles, California,
1996

Client
Jim and Maria Hardy

Architect
Lubowicki/Lanier
Architects: Susan Lanier

Structural Engineers
Parker/Resnick Structural
Engineers

Mechanical Engineers
William Comeau

General Contractor
Kent Snyder Construction

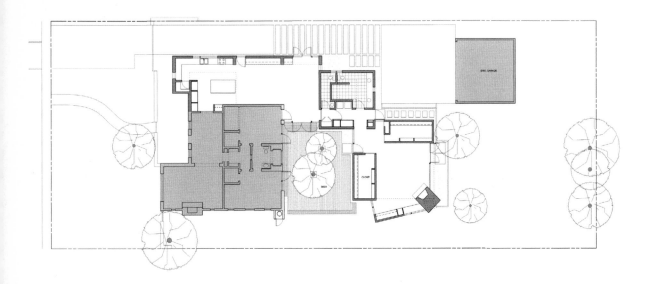

BRIAN MACKAY-LYONS
ARCHITECTURE URBAN DESIGN

Principal	Brian MacKay-Lyons
Born	1954
Education	Dalhousie University, 1972
	Technical University of Nova Scotia, 1978
	University of California, Los Angeles, 1982
	International Laboratory for Architecture and Urban Design, 1982
Work	W. Brian Edwards Architect, 1977
	Networks, 1978–80
	Urban Innovations Group, 1980–82
	Moore Ruble Yudell, 1982
	Emodi and MacKay-Lyons Architects, 1983–85
	Brian MacKay-Lyons Architecture Urban Design, 1985–
Teaching	Professor, Dalhousie University Faculty of Architecture, 1997– ; Assistant Professor, 1983–89; Associate Professor, 1989–97
	Visiting Professor, Auburn University, winter 2001
	Thomas H. Bullock Chair, Texas A & M University, winter 2001
Prizes	Heritage Canada Restoration Award, 1986
	Governor General's Medal for Architecture, 1986, 1992, 1997
	Nova Scotia Association of Architects Medal of Excellence, 1987
	Prix de Rome, 1987
	Canadian Architect Award of Excellence, 1988, 1993, 1996, 1998
	Lieutenant Governor's Medal of Excellence, 1990, 1991, 1993, 1995
Exhibitions	"Ten Shades of Green," Architectural League of New York, 2000
	Brian MacKay-Lyons traveling exhibition, 2000–2001
	Brian MacKay-Lyons European traveling exhibition, 2001

SHIM-SUTCLIFFE ARCHITECTS

Principal	Brigitte Shim
Born	1958
Education	University of Waterloo, 1981, 1983
Work	Arthur Erickson and Associates, 1983
	Baird/Sampson Architects, 1983–87
	Shim-Sutcliffe Architects, 1992–
Teaching	Instructor, University of Toronto, 1988–2002
	Visiting Professor, Harvard Graduate School of Design, 1993, 1996
	Bishop Visiting Professor, Yale University, 2001
	Visiting Professor, Ecole Polytechnique Fédérale de Lausanne, 2002

Principal	Howard Sutcliffe
Born	1958
Education	University of Waterloo, 1981, 1983
Work	Ronald Thom Architect, 1983–85
	Barton Myers Architect, 1985–87
	KPMB Architects, 1987–94
	Shim-Sutcliffe Architects, 1992–
Prizes	Governor General's Medal for Architecture, 1994, 1997, 1999
	American Wood Council Design Award, 1996
	Canadian Wood Council Design Award, 1998
Exhibitions	P/A Design Awards, Rensselaer Polytechnic Institute, Troy, New York, 1999
	La Biennale 2000 de Montreal, Centre International d'Art Contemporain de Montreal, 2000
	"Transform(ing) Chicago's Design Competition for Mixed Income Housing," Harold Washington Library, Chicago, 2001

WENDELL BURNETTE ARCHITECTS

Principal	Wendell Burnette
Born	1962
Education	Taliesin West, Frank Lloyd Wright School of Architecture, 1980–83
Work	William Mims Associates, 1983–85 William P. Bruder Architect, 1985–96 Wendell Burnette Architects, 1996–
Teaching	Assistant Professor, Arizona State University College of Architecture, 2000; Adjunct Faculty, 1997; Faculty Associate, 1999
Prizes	Record Houses Award, *Architectural Record* Magazine, 1996, 2000 Emerging Voices Award, Architectural League of New York, 1999 P/A Design Awards, 1999 Honor Award, Arizona Masonry Guild, 2000 Home of the Year Merit Award, Arizona AIA, 2000
Exhibitions	"Design Culture Now," National Design Triennial, Cooper Hewitt National Design Museum, 2000

RICK JOY ARCHITECTS

Principal	Rick Joy
Born	1958
Education	University of Maine, 1978 Portland School of Art, 1984 University of Arizona, 1990
Work	William P. Bruder Architect, 1990–92 Rick Joy Architect, 1993–
Teaching	Visiting Professor, Harvard Graduate School of Design, fall 2000
Prizes	Young Architects Award, *Progressive Architecture* Magazine, 1993 Design Distinction, Environments, *I.D.* Magazine Annual Design Awards, 1997, 2000 Arizona Home of the Year, AIA Central Arizona Chapter, 2000 Commendation, AR+D Emerging Architecture Awards, 2000 Record Houses Award, *Architectural Record* Magazine, 2001
Exhibitions	Young Architects Forum, Architectural League of New York, 1996 GA Gallery: Tokyo GA Houses Projects, 1999, 2000 "Ten Shades of Green," Architectural League of New York, 2000 "The Works," Montana State University, 2000

WESLEY WEI ARCHITECTS

Principal   Wesley Wei

Born   1953

Education   Pennsylvania State University, 1976
              University of Pennsylvania, 1977

Work   Mitchell/Giurgola Architects, 1976
              Venturi and Rauch Architects
              and Planners, 1977
              Robert L Decker & H2L2 Design, 1977–79,
              1980–86
              Wesley Wei Architects, 1987–

Teaching   Associate Professor, Pennsylvania State
              University, 1981–87
              Visiting Professor, Temple University, 1987–89,
              1991–92
              Visiting Professor, Rhode Island School of
              Design, 1989
              Lecturer, University of Pennsylvania, 1992–

Prizes   Young Architects Award, AIA Philadelphia, 1989
              American Academy in Rome Prize, 1994
              Design Award, AIA Pennsylvania, 1997
              Open Plan Award, Pennsylvania Society of
              Architects, 1998
              Honor Award, AIA Philadelphia, 1999
              Gold Medal Award, AIA Philadelphia, 2000
              Record Houses Award, *Architectural Record*
              Magazine, 2001

Exhibitions   "Philadelphia Architects," Thirty-eighth Annual
              American Contemporary Art Exhibition,
              Lehigh University, 1994
              "Figure/Frame/Shadow + The Architectural
              Program," Graduate School of Fine Arts,
              University of Pennsylvania, 1994
              "Wesley Wei Architect, Domestic Work: Recent
              Projects," FAARM, 2000

SHoP: SHARPLES HOLDEN PASQUARELLI

Principal	Christopher Sharples
Born	1963
Education	Dickinson College, 1987 Columbia University, 1990
Work	Aoshima Sekkei Architects, 1990–94 Sharples Design, 1994–96 SHoP, 1996–
Teaching	Interior Design Department, Parsons School of Design, New York, 1996–99 Adjunct Professor, School of Architecture, Urban Design and Landscape Architecture, City College, City University of New York, 2000, 2002

Principal	William Sharples
Born	1963
Education	Pennsylvania State University, 1988 Columbia University, 1994
Work	Peter Lynch Architect, 1992–97 Sharples Design, 1994–96 SHoP, 1996–
Teaching	Parsons School of Design, 1996–99

Principal	Coren Sharples
Born	1965
Education	College of Business and Management, University of Maryland, 1987 Columbia University, 1994
Work	Rafael Viñoly Architects, 1994 Sharples Design, 1994–96 Hone & Associates, 1994–97 SHoP, 1996–

Principal	Kimberly Holden
Born	1966
Education	University of Vermont, 1988 Columbia University, 1994
Work	Greg Lynn FORM and Michael McInturf Architects, 1994–96 Holden Pasquarelli Design, 1994–97 Hanrahan + Meyers Architects, 1996 John Ciardullo Associates, 1997–98 SHoP, 1996–

Principal	Gregg Pasquarelli
Born	1965
Education	Villanova University, 1987 Columbia University, 1994
Work	Greg Lynn FORM and Michael McInturf Architects, 1994–98 SHoP, 1996–
Teaching	Adjunct Assistant Professor, Columbia University, 1995–
Prizes	Emerging Voices Award, Architectural League of New York, 2001 Academy Award in Architecture, American Academy of Arts and Letters, 2001
Exhibitions	Young Architects Program, Museum of Modern Art/P.S.1, 2000 "Folds, Blobs, and Boxes," Carnegie Museum of Art, 2001 "The Programmable City," Storefront for Art and Architecture, 2001 "Do You Really Want Another Style?" American Academy of Arts and Letters, Parsons School of Design, University of Pennsylvania, 2001

KUTH/RANIERI ARCHITECTS

Principal	Byron Kuth
Born	1953
Education	Rhode Island School of Design, 1985, 1986
Work	Kuth/Ranieri Architects, 1992–
Teaching	California College of Arts and Crafts, 1987– Instructor, Harvard Graduate School of Design, 1999

Principal	Elizabeth Ranieri
Born	1963
Education	Rhode Island School of Design, 1986
Work	Kuth/Ranieri Architects, 1992–
Teaching	Adjunct Professor, California College of Arts and Crafts, 1989 Instructor, Harvard Graduate School of Design, 1999

Prizes	Young Architects Award, Architectural League of New York, 1994 Honor Award, AIA California State, 1994 Honor Award, National AIA, 1994 Best of Category, Environments, *I.D.* Magazine Annual Design Awards, 1999

Exhibitions	Young Architects Forum, Architectural League of New York, 1994 "Fabrications," San Francisco Museum of Modern Art, 1997–98 "2 x 2: Architectural Collaborations," University of California, Berkeley, Art Museum and Pacific Film Archive, 2000 "Recent Work," Harvard Graduate School of Design, 2000

LUBOWICKI/LANIER ARCHITECTS

Principal	Paul Lubowicki
Born	1954
Education	Cooper Union, 1977
Work	Raimund Abraham, Architect, 1977
	Frank O. Gehry & Associates, 1977–84
	Paul Lubowicki, Architect, 1986–88
	Lubowicki/Lanier Architects, 1988–
Teaching	Instructor, UCLA Graduate School of Design, 1985
	Instructor, Harvard Graduate School of Design, 1985, 1994
	Instructor, Yale University Graduate School of Architecture, 1986–89
	Instructor, Southern California Institute of Architecture, 1986–94, 1996–97
	Instructor, University of Texas at Arlington, 1997
	Design Studio Instructor, Tulane School of Architecture, 2001, 2002

Principal	Susan Lanier
Born	1949
Education	Pitzer College, 1971
	Southern California Institute of Architecture, 1988
Work	Morphosis, 1985–87
	Lubowicki/Lanier Architects, 1988–
Teaching	Instructor, Southern California Institute of Architecture, 1990–92, 1996–99
	Instructor, Harvard Graduate School of Design, 1994
	Instructor, University of Southern California School of Architecture, 1995–96, 1997
	Instructor, University of Texas at Arlington, 1997
	Design Studio Instructor, Tulane School of Architecture, 2001, 2002

Prizes	Honor Award, AIA Los Angeles Chapter, 1998
	Interiors Award, *Architectural Record* Magazine, 1994
	Record Houses Award, *Architectural Record* Magazine, 1994
Exhibitions	"Angels & Franciscans: Innovative Architecture from Los Angeles and San Francisco," Gagosian Gallery, 1992–93
	"Southland Revision: A New Generation of Contemporary Regional Architecture," 1995
	"Architecture in Balance: 7 Southern Californian Architects," Armory Center for the Arts, 1997
	"98 WATTS," UCLA Department of Architecture and Urban Design, 1998
	"New Blood 101: Turning Point," Pacific Design Center, 1998–99

ABOUT THE AUTHORS

Susanna Sirefman has been an adjunct professor of architecture
at the School of Architecture, Urban Design and Landscape
Architecture at City College, City University of New York, since
1997. She has also taught at Parsons School of Design and has
been a visiting critic at the University of North London, the Art
Institute of Chicago School of Interior Architecture, Columbia
University, Yale University, Cooper Union, and the Pratt Institute.
Her design work has been featured in *Abitare* and *Interior Design*
and won the Second Annual IIDA Residential Design Competition
1999. Sirefman is the author of several books, including *New York:
A Guide to Recent Architecture* and *Chicago: A Guide to Recent
Architecture*, and has contributed to *Architecture, Architectural
Record, Metropolis, Graphis,* and *Daedalus: Journal of the American
Academy of Arts and Sciences*, among other publications.

George Ranalli is dean of the School of Architecture, Urban Design
and Landscape Architecture at City College, City University
of New York. Previously, he was a professor of architecture at Yale
University. His work has been featured in *Domus, A+U, Progressive
Architecture,* and *Lotus,* among many other international publications, and in the monograph *George Ranalli: Buildings and Projects*,
and is represented in the permanent collection of New York's
Museum of Modern Art. Ranalli has designed installations for
exhibitions at the Whitney Museum, on the work of Frank Lloyd
Wright, and at the Canadian Centre for Architecture, on the
work of Carlo Scarpa. He has lectured at schools of architecture,
museums, and art organizations around the world.

Michael Sorkin is director of the Graduate Urban Design Program
at City College, City University of New York. His design practice,
Michael Sorkin Studio, is devoted to practical and theoretical
projects at all scales, with a special interest in the city. His recent
projects include master planning in Hamburg and Schwerin,
Germany, planning for a Palestinian capital in East Jerusalem, and
studies of the Manhattan waterfront and Far Rockaway. Sorkin is
a noted author and critic; his books include *Variations on a Theme
Park* (1991), *Michael Sorkin Studio: Wiggle* (1998), *Some Assembly
Required* (2001), and *The Next Jerusalem* (2003), and he was for
many years the architecture critic of the *Village Voice*.